# Rhetoric and American Statesmanship

# Rhetoric and American Statesmanship

edited by

Glen E. Thurow
and
Jeffrey D. Wallin

CAROLINA ACADEMIC PRESS
and
THE CLAREMONT INSTITUTE FOR THE STUDY OF
STATESMANSHIP AND POLITICAL PHILOSOPHY

Carolina Academic Press
Post Office Box 8795
Forest Hills Station
Durham, NC 27707

© Glen E. Thurow and Jeffrey D. Wallin
First Published 1984

Library of Congress Catalogue Card Number 83-70310
ISBN 0-89089-254-7 (cloth)
ISBN 0-89089-255-5 (paper)

# TABLE OF CONTENTS

# FOREWORD

The authors of this collection were participants, as speakers or discussants, at a conference on "Rhetoric and Statesmanship" held at the University of Dallas in October 1980.

The conference was cosponsored by the Department of Politics at the University of Dallas and the Intercollegiate Studies Institute, Inc. We are grateful for the Institute's generous support.

# CONTRIBUTORS

LARRY P. ARNN
is Vice-President of Public Research, Syndicated and Secretary of The Claremont Institute for the Study of Statesmanship and Political Philosophy. He is a D.Phil. candidate at Worcester College, Oxford, and a Ph.D. candidate in political philosophy and American government at Claremont Graduate School. For three years, he served as Research Assistant to Martin Gilbert, the official biographer of Winston Churchill. He has contributed articles to *Grand Strategy: Countercurrents* and has published widely in the press on British and international politics.

WALTER BERNS
is a Resident Scholar of the American Enterprise Institute. He has published in numerous journals, popular as well as scholarly, and his several books on the American Constitution and American politics include, most recently, *For Capital Punishment: Crime and the Morality of the Death Penalty* (1979).

EVA T. H. BRANN
holds the Addison E. Millikin tutorship at St. John's College. She is author of *Paradoxes of Education in a Republic* (1979), of a book on Late Geometric and Protoattic pottery, and of numerous articles.

HARVEY C. MANSFIELD, JR.
is Professor of Government at Harvard University. He is author of several books, including *The Spirit of Liberalism* (1978) and *Machiavelli's New Modes and Orders: A Study of the Discourses on Livy* (1979), and has published widely on political philosophy and American politics.

FORREST MCDONALD
is Professor of History and Distinguished Senior Fellow of the Center for the Study of Southern History and Culture at the University of Alabama. He is the author of many books and articles on American history, including *Alexander Hamilton: A Biography* (1979) and *A Constitutional History of the United States* (1982).

THOMAS B. SILVER
is President of Public Research, Syndicated and a Resident Fellow of The Claremont Institute for the Study of Statesmanship and Political

Philosophy. He is author of *Coolidge and the Historians* (1982), has published in *The American Scholar*, and has written extensively in the press on politics and economics.

GLEN E. THUROW

is an Associate Professor and Chairman of the Department of Politics at the University of Dallas. He is author of *Abraham Lincoln and American Political Religion* (1976) and has published in *Political Theory, Interpretation, Presidential Studies Quarterly, St. Mary's Law Journal,* and elsewhere.

JEFFREY TULIS

is Assistant Professor of Political Science at Princeton University. His studies of the American presidency and presidential rhetoric have appeared in several journals and anthologies. He is co-editor of *The Presidency in the Constitutional Order* (1981).

JEFFREY D. WALLIN

is an Associate Professor of Politics at the University of Dallas. He is currently on leave from the University of Dallas and is Director of the Division of General Programs at the National Endowment for the Humanities. He is author of *By Ships Alone: Churchill and the Dardanelles* (1980) and articles on British and American statesmanship.

JOHN ZVESPER

is a Lecturer in Politics at the University of East Anglia. Holder of degrees from Claremont Men's College and Cambridge, he is the author of *Political Philosophy and Rhetoric: A Study of the Origins of American Party Politics* (1977).

# Rhetoric and American Statesmanship

# INTRODUCTION

*In this and like communities, public sentiment is everything. With public sentiment, nothing can fail; without it, nothing can succeed. Consequently, he who moulds public sentiment goes deeper than he who enacts statutes or pronounces decisions. He makes statutes and decisions possible or impossible to be executed.*

Abraham Lincoln

It is no accident that the two greatest defenders of modern democratic civilization, Abraham Lincoln and Winston Churchill, have also been her greatest rhetoricians. Lincoln's lucid and moving prose defined for a heated nation the momentous issues involved in the extension of slavery, led it through the perils of civil war, and helped to forge anew the bonds of union—bonds vital to the United States and other free nations as well. Winston Churchill's defiant and indomitable words aroused the dormant spirit of the West at a time when, quite simply, it was threatened with destruction. In both, forming and moving public opinion was essential to their abilities to meet the great crises they and democracy faced.

Governments that rest upon the consent of the governed find their possibilities and their limits in the opinions which rule the public. Political institutions may slow the workings of public sentiment, giving people time for second thoughts and statesmen time to exercise some discretion, but in the end, as Tocqueville noted, "the opinions, prejudices, interests, and even passions of the people can find no lasting obstacles." To shape public opinion is to shape the ruling authority in governments such as ours.

Rhetoric is the name that has been traditionally given to the kind of speech which is effective in moulding public sentiment. Not every kind of speech can persuade the public at large. A learned treatise containing a long and complicated chain of reasoning resting upon obscure observations may excite the admiration of a scholarly convention, but spoken before a mass meeting arouses only laughter, boredom, outrage, or contempt. The study of rhetoric attempts to discover what it is that makes speech politically effective, in what ways this kind of speech is like other kinds of speech, and in what ways it differs. Good public speaking is essential for a good democracy, and an understanding of its nature and limits is essential for understanding democratic statesmanship.

Today democracy stands sorely in need of an effective public presentation of the opinions upon which it rests. The fundamental public sentiment that makes possible democratic statutes and decisions is under attack from abroad and threatened with erosion from within. The vast majority of the world, both

Communist and non-Communist, is ruled by opinions profoundly anti-democratic in character. Finding themselves in a sea of hostile opinion, the leaders of
the democratic nations have even been willing to defend their policies in international forums using the language and principles of countries and movements
whose goal is the destruction of democratic man. Because they have not recognized the importance of forming fundamental sentiments, the war has been
conceded in seeking to win the immediate battle.

But it would be easier for statesmen to develop a successful strategy to
counter the strength of anti-democratic opinion in the world at large were it not
for the erosion within. The problems of governing their own countries have
grown more intractable as the principles of republican government, around
which men might rally, have been forgotten because they are seldom adequately
recalled and defended. Indeed, without politically effective speech that can
both tap and form liberal democratic opinion, speech itself seems to lose its
restorative powers. Today, the media, scholars, and general public alike are
beset by doubts that the speech of our elected officials is trustworthy, that
it contains any noteworthy understanding of the country's purposes and difficulties, or that it has any effect on what is done. Cynicism about public
speech leads our TV commentators and others not to ask, Does the speech make
sense?, but, Which ethnic group is the official trying to appeal to now? Whose
interest or greed is he secretly serving? What psychological motive would make
him say such a thing? The undoubted truth that politicians sometimes have
interests not identical with those of the public is generalized into the dogma
that a statesman's words are but a rationalization for his actions, or a screen
behind which he can carry out deeds he could not defend in public. This increasingly pervasive view holds that speech cannot be seen as a genuine attempt
to deliberate about, or to express, the common good.

The cynicism now so pervasive undermines the American tradition of
respect for speech—it undermines our ability to govern ourselves by means of
discussion and argument, rather than by tricks and force. Cynicism is a self-
fulfilling prophecy. For if people do not think that the speeches of our statesmen
reflect serious deliberation about the common good and significantly affect the
choices made, then speeches will not be of this character—at least not in
the long run—for speakers will take no care to make good arguments and
citizens will not bother to listen. Ambitious men will become willing to say
anything that will enhance their own position, because they think that words
are but weapons.

These corroding effects are visible in the increasing role of image–making,
mood-appeals, and other techniques of modern advertising in political speech to
the exclusion of serious discussion of issues and policies. The chief spokesmen
of modern advertising now find themselves elevated to positions within the White
House itself. From them, statesmen learn how to sell their "images" by pleasing

and flattering their audiences. There are many nations in the world—indeed, even the majority of nations—that do not have the respect for speech that has been traditional in the United States, and their governments only too clearly reflect what is necessary to govern such nations.

Yet for all the necessity of a good rhetoric in today's democracies, the term "rhetoric" has an oddly archaic sound. Departments of rhetoric have been replaced in our universities by departments of communication, and in popular usage the term is used almost solely in a pejorative sense to dismiss overblown or hackneyed oratory—"mere rhetoric." The transformation of "rhetoric" into an archaic or pejorative word and its replacement by "communication" is due to a loss in understanding of the problem of political speech.

The central problem of democratic speech is not that there may be a lack of communication between people, to be remedied by better communication. The Nazi may communicate or feel at one with his fellow Nazi even as the democratic citizen may communicate or feel at one with his fellow citizen. The crucial political question is not whether one communicates, but whether one communicates by sharing Nazi or democratic principles and sentiments. Dogs, cats, and even insects "communicate," for communication need not take place by means of speech. A bark, meow, or buzz—or touch, sniff, or gesture—may bring animals or humans into communion, and our media of communication may work as much by picture and sound as by speech. But it is only speech—only rhetoric —that can connect men to the principles and sentiments that make democratic government possible. Only speech can distinguish democratic from Nazi principles, and only rhetoric can effectively make that distinction in political life. Communication replaces rhetoric when men forget or ignore the difference between freedom and slavery.

It is because this difference is ignored that rhetoric can come to be understood as mastery of the techniques for pleasing and flattering audiences and advertising men can become the teachers of public speaking. In contrast, Lincoln learned his rhetoric from Shakespeare, the King James Bible, and a tradition of rhetorical education stretching back to Plato and Aristotle, a tradition important in the formation of American statesmen generally until the twentieth century. This tradition taught that true rhetoric must serve political knowledge, not merely the opinions of the crowd, and must possess an understanding of human beings that enables it both to persuade effectively and to improve men, not merely to flatter them.

A political speaker never aims, like a pedagogue or an entertainer, simply to instruct or amuse his audience. He wants to move it, to stir it to action, to gain its acquiescence, or to check it from some undesired course. When a political man does entertain or instruct his audience, it is usually because he needs first to attract or teach them in order to move them in the direction he intends. Even the best examples of instructive or beautiful political rhetoric reflect in some measure the subordination of these qualities to action. The *Federalist Papers* offers instruction in the principles of republican government, but for the immediate purpose of winning ratification of the Constitution and, perhaps, the long-range purpose of securing the rule of a particular interpretation of the Constitution. The "Gettysburg Address" approaches poetry in its precision and beauty of language, but its poetry elevates in order to attach men more firmly to the Union and "government of the people, by the people, for the people."

The ability of a speaker to move his audience depends in part on the character of his audience. The resources a speaker has at his command vary as audiences vary. Some men, for example, may be wary of any speaker who does not look, dress, and speak like themselves; others may appreciate a wider range of human types. Some groups of men may be susceptible to impassioned appeals to patriotism; others may only be embarassed. Some may be accustomed to following complicated arguments; others may stumble at a single syllogism. The character of the audience limits, if it does not define, the persuasive powers of the speaker. Effective political speech, then, must bend itself to its audience.

Yet political speech cannot be judged solely by how well it appeals to its audience. Political speech must serve the ends of statesmanship. Abraham Lincoln is acknowledged to be the greatest speaker ever to hold the office of President of the United States. His failure to persuade his audience on occasion shows why successful persuasion cannot be the sole measure of proper rhetoric. In his First Inaugural Address, he tried to persuade the South that it should not secede from the Union. The speech failed. Was it, therefore, a bad speech? It is difficult to think of what else Lincoln might have said, or how else he might have said it, that would have succeeded, short of giving in on the issue of the extension of slavery. Lincoln's goal, a Union agreed that, in principle, slavery was contrary to the country's moral foundations, was a goal that a significant portion of the Union could not be persuaded to adopt in 1861. Was it therefore an improper goal, because beyond the reach of rhetoric to achieve? To say so for this reason alone would be like saying that one should not make laws against murder because not everyone can be persuaded not to murder. Properly governing men may require the use of the force of police and armies as well as the persuasion of speakers. Rhetoric may be in the service of a goal that is beyond the reach of rhetoric alone to achieve.

These reflections mean that the test of good democratic rhetoric cannot simply be the success of its appeal to an audience. While good rhetoric aims to appeal to its audience, it must serve ends which are not those of simply pleasing its hearers. The challenge of rhetoric is to bridge the gap between what the common good requires and what an unpersuaded audience would permit. It succeeds by moving the audience as much as it can be moved, which may not be sufficient. It is true that politics is the art of the possible. A politics which aims at the impossible may be morally blameable, but the possible is not limited solely by the possibilities of rhetoric. Yet a country that can be moved to the common good by the persuasion of its leaders is surely preferable to one in which force must be used.

The purpose of this book is to recapture and examine the older tradition of republican rhetoric and to contrast it with the rhetoric dominating our public life today. To recapture this older tradition does not mean to pick up some body of knowledge which lies neglected, but to recapture an understanding of the problem of political speech in democratic societies in light of the political principles which underlie them.

Four of the essays in this book examine the tradition of republican rhetoric in the light cast by four of the great masters of that rhetoric. Eva Brann shows how James Madison's *Memorial and Remonstrance* was able to combine an unbending adherence to the truth with a powerful and lastingly effective appeal to his audience. Forrest McDonald analyzes how Alexander Hamilton was able to marshal arguments into some of the most effective polemics in history, while letting us see as well how that skill served the aims of a comprehensive statesmanship. Thomas Silver uncovers the rhetoric of Calvin Coolidge, long hidden by the partisanship of historians, and reveals how the rhetorical tradition of the American founders could be continued in greatly changed circumstances. Winston Churchill is shown by Larry Arnn to be acutely aware of the problematic character of rhetoric and yet to have good reasons for regarding it as at the center of the statesman's task.

Two of the essays examine the change from the older to the newer understanding of rhetoric. Jeffrey Tulis traces this change in the context of the Presidency from the 19th to the 20th centuries, and reflects upon its causes and justification. John Zvesper offers an assessment of the New Deal oratory of Franklin Roosevelt and the changes it brought to American political speech.

The final two essays assess the rhetoric dominating our contemporary situation. Walter Berns describes the failure of current judicial rhetoric to serve the law and our political order more generally. Harvey Mansfield, Jr., examines the character of the rhetoric fostered by the modern media, and the tension between that rhetoric and sound republican principles.

The essays as a whole thus provide a basis for assessing American rhetoric today and the alternative to it found in our democratic traditions.

GLEN E. THUROW
UNIVERSITY OF DALLAS

# 1

# MADISON'S "MEMORIAL AND REMONSTRANCE"

## A Model of American Eloquence

### EVA T. H. BRANN

The document entitled "To the Honorable the General Assembly of the Commonwealth of Virginia, A Memorial and Remonstrance" is a jewel of republican rhetoric.[1] Nor has this choice example of American eloquence gone without notice. And yet, compared to the Declaration of Independence and the Gettysburg Address, it has remained obscure—more often quarried for stately phrases than conned by heart, more often admired at a distance than studied in detail. This lack of popularity can in part be accounted for by the circumstances of the document. Addressed to the legislature of a state rather than to the people of the nation, it is concerned with an issue which is critical only sporadically, though then critical indeed. The Supreme Court has, to be sure, searched the document on several occasions for help in interpreting the "establishment" clause of the First Amendment. (See the Appendix.) But this naturally narrow judicial mining of the text has itself served to draw away attention from the depth of its political precepts and the fitness of its rhetorical form, discerningly lauded,

---

1. Printed with introduction and notes in *The Papers of James Madison*, Robert A. Rutland and William M. E. Rachal, eds., (Chicago) Vol. 8 (1784–1786), pp. 295–306. I know of no detailed study of the Remonstrance.

for example, by Rives, Madison's nineteenth century biographer.[2] In part, again, Madison's work has been kept off the roster of canonized public prose because it lacks Jefferson's heady generalities and Lincoln's humane grandeur. But I know this: To study it is to come away with a sense of having discovered, under the veil of Madison's modesty, the great rhetorician of the Founding, whom John Marshall called "the most eloquent man I ever heard." The immediate and the historical efficacy of Madison's appeal shows that despite the deprecating modern estimate that he "could not mesmerize a mass audience" but "only those who sought ... illumination,"[3] Madison was master of that true eloquence which sometimes turns the former kind of audience into the latter. It is an eloquence of measured passion and sober ardor, which knows what to say when and to whom without bending the truth.

# I. The Circumstances Surrounding the Remonstrance[4]

On December 3, 1784, a bill "establishing a provision for Teachers of Religion" was reported to the General Assembly of Virginia. Its preamble said:

Whereas the general diffusion of Christian knowledge hath a natural tendency to correct the morals of men, restrain their vices, and preserve the peace of

---

2. William Cabell Rives, A *History of the Life and Times of James Madison* (Boston 1859), p. 632:
   > In this masterly paper, he discussed the question of an establishment of religion by law from every point of view, —of natural right, the inherent limitations of the civil power, the interests of religion itself, the genius and precepts of Christianity, the warning lessons of history, the dictates of a wise and sober policy,—and treated them all with a consummate power of reasoning, and a force of appeal to the understandings and hearts of people, that bore down every opposing prejudice and precluded reply.
   "This noble production of the mind and heart of Mr. Madison" is, he concluded this perfectly just appreciation, a triumphant plea in the great cause of religious liberty, "never surpassed in power or eloquence by any which its stirring influence have called forth."
3. Neal Riemer, *James Madison* (New York 1968), pp. 12–13. Riemer does not rate Madison's rhetorical gifts very high, particularly when compared to those of Jefferson and of Paine. He describes the style as earnest, forthright, simple, unadorned, quiet. "His writings convince but do not take fire." I think his estimate too much reduces rhetoric to oratory.
4. Sources: *Papers*, Vol 8, pp. 295–98; Madison's "Detached Memoranda" in the *William and Mary Quarterly*, Third Series, III, (October 1946, pp. 555–56; Irving Brant, *James Madison* 1, Vol. 2, *The Nationalist; 1780–1787* New York 1948), pp. 343–55; Charles F. James, *Documentary History of the Struggle for Religious Liberty* (New York 1971), pp. 128–41; Ralph Ketcham, *James Madison* (London 1971), pp. 162–68; Anson Phelps Stokes, *Church and State in the United States*, Vol. I (New York 1950), pp. 339–45; Manfred Zippers, *Thomas Jefferson's "Acr for Establishing Religious Freedom in Virginia" vom 16. Januar 1786*, Dissertation (Erlangen 1967), pp. 24–28.

society, which cannot be effected without a competent provision for learned teachers, who may be thereby enabled to devote their time and attention to the duty of instructing such citizens as from their circumstances and want of education cannot otherwise attain such knowledge; and it is judged such provision may be made by the Legislature, without counteracting the liberal principle heretofore adopted and intended to be preserved, by abolishing all distinctions of pre-eminence amongst the different societies or communities of Christians. . . .[5]

The author of the bill, Patrick Henry, had introduced it with a fervent speech tracing the downfall of ancient and modern polities to the decay of religion: the repeal in 1776 of the tithe law, which meant the end of a state-salaried clergy and amounted to the disestablishment of the Anglican Church, was a source of such decay in Virginia. Other eminent Virginians, even more anxious about an increase in laxness of morals and lawlessness than about the precipitous decline of church attendance during and after the Revolution, saw nothing wrong with the bill. Among them were George Washington and John Marshall.

Madison, absolutely opposed, debated Henry on the floor of the Assembly late in November. These speeches contain revealing anticipations of—and contrasts to—the Remonstrance.[6]

Even with the bill still in committee, Madison's arguments had told. There had been a short-lived attempt to de-christianize it by extending it to all "who profess the public worship of the Deity," be they Mohametans or Jews. The bill reported out was, furthermore, no longer the General Assessment bill which had sought in effect to re-establish Christianity (though, of course, not Anglicanism) by a general levy on taxpayers in support of a Christian church. It had been transformed into a Christian education bill, designed partly, as evidenced by the reference in the preamble to those who cannot afford private education, to be a defense against Jefferson's long tabled secular public education bill of 1779, and partly, as is apparent from its more restricted aims, to be a response to Madison's pressure.

Meanwhile Madison also engaged in some practical politics. In order to remove the oratorical Henry from the scene, Madison had hit on a device both kinder and more efficacious than Jefferson's suggestion "devotedly to pray for his death": he had conspired to elevate him to the governorship. The proud governor-elect had retired to his estates, "a circumstance very inauspicious to his offspring" as Madison wrote with satisfaction to James Monroe.

Also, in exchange for the withdrawal of his opposition to a companion bill for the incorporation of the Episcopal Church, Madison had won postponement of final action on the bill to 1785, so that there might be time to publish its text for consideration by the people. This move was crucial, since in 1784 the bill would

---

5. James, p. 129.
6. The speeches are extant in the form of notes; see *Papers*, Vol. 8, pp. 195–99.

probably have passed the legislature with an overwhelming majority.[7] Here as ever, the two facets of Madison's statesmanship—practical maneuvering and principled rhetoric—complemented each other. He had gained a year.

Throughout the spring of 1785 Madison's own inclination was to wait quietly for the popular opposition to manifest itself. The Episcopalians, as old beneficiaries of establishment naturally, and the Presbyterian clergy to their shame, supported the bill; the laity and clergy of the dissenting sects were solidly opposed. By May several supporters, but no opponents, of the bill had lost their seats. As late as June 21 Madison was assured enough of its unpopularity merely to echo the rebellious common feeling, that although the legislature "should give it the *form*, they will not give it the *validity* of a law …—I own the bill appears to me to warrant this language of the people."[8]

Some of his associates in the battle, however, George Mason and the brothers Nicholas, were anxious for more pointed action. They had reason to fear civil disturbances if the legislature, in which the favoring tidewater counties were overrepresented, should attempt to force the law on the people. They hoped to deter its passage with a large number of well-subscribed identical petitions from all parts of the state, the best device then available for conveying the power of a public sentiment to the legislature. They asked Madison to compose the text.

He wrote the "Memorial and Remonstrance" sometime soon after June 20, 1785, intending it to circulate anonymously. The few friends who knew of his authorship respected his wish, which arose, presumably, from his desire to maintain good working relations with all parties in the legislature. At the time some attributed the work to George Mason, who had drafted the religious liberty clause of the Virginia Declaration of Rights. Though a printer had put his name on a reprint as early as 1786, Madison acknowledged only late in life, in a letter of 1826 to Mason's grandson, that "the task of composing such a paper had been imposed upon him."

Mason had the petition printed as a broadside in Alexandria, having seen no reason for changing even one word of the text. The Nicholases saw to its distribution throughout the state. It met, Madison noted in retrospect, "with the approbation of the Baptists, the Presbyterians [who had recanted], the Quakers, and the few Roman Catholics, universally; of the Methodists in part; and even of not a few of the Sect formerly established by law [the Episcopalians]."[9]

The Remonstrance was solidly successful in drawing subscribers. The thirteen circulated copies collected 1552 signatures; 150 freeholders signed one

7. Gaillard Hunt, "Madison and Religious Liberty," *Annual Report of the American Historical Association* (1901), Vol. I, p. 168.
8. Rives, p. 631.
9. "Detached Memoranda," pp. 555–56.

petition in a day. Yet, successful though it was, another, still anonymous, petition, based on the fervently Christian argument that the bill contravened the spirit of the Gospel, ran up more than three times as many signatures on twenty-nine copies. All in all, about eighty opposing petitions with 10,929 signatures came in to Richmond, and only a few in support.

After a brief consideration the bill died in committee in the fall of 1785, lost, however, by a mere three votes. Madison's petition may well have been crucial.

On January 22, 1786, Madison reported the results of that session to Jefferson in Paris in a modestly jubilant vein:

The steps taken throughout the Country to defeat the Gnl. Assessment, had produced all the effect that could have been wished. The table was loaded with petitions and remonstrances from all parts against the interposition of the Legislature in matters of Religion.

In the same letter he had already told Jefferson even greater news. One element alone of Jefferson's six-year-old revisal of the laws of Virginia had that year been passed into an act, his bill for establishing religious freedom,[10] the most celebrated of all documents concerned with religious liberty.

Advantage had been taken of the crisis produced by the crushing of the religious assessment bill to carry through the Jefferson bill, as Madison put it. The two events were closely connected. The impetus of the collapse of a regressive measure carried over—as sometimes happens—into a sudden advance. The religious clause of the Virginia Declaration of Rights had guaranteed the free exercise of religion to all Christians, but it had not unequivocally banned—witness the assessment bill—the establishment of a non-sectarian state church. During the next nine years the legislature had passed a patchwork of special exemptions, tolerances, and particular measures favoring dissenting sects. Jefferson's bill, which happened to attack compulsory support of religious teachers in its preamble, rode in, as Madison recollected in 1826, under the "influence of public sentiment" manifested in the death of the assessment bill, as a "permanent Barrier agst. future attempts on the Rights of Conscience as declared in the Great Charter affixed to the Constitution of the State."[11] Madison interpreted the petitions against the assessment bill as demands for the enactment of Jefferson's law concerning religious freedom; he thought it an advantage that it had been sanctioned by what was in effect a plebiscite. The Remonstrance had advanced it as a principle that there should be such invitations to the people to express their sentiments in the course of lawmaking.

10. *Papers*, Vol. 8, p. 473.
11. *Papers*, Vol. 8, p. 298.

# II. The Arguments of the Remonstrance

The Remonstrance is a petition addressed to the General Assembly of Virginia that remonstrates on fifteen counts (listed in summary in Note 12) against a bill before it establishing a provision for teachers of the Christian religion. Each of these points is set forth in one paragraph in the form of a reflection on one aspect of the right relation between religion and politics. Madison clearly intended to make the argumentation as complete, as principled, as fundamental, and yet as concise as possible.

The fifteen counts are, furthermore, composed into a symmetrical structure. The eighth, that is, the middle point, addresses the concern immediately central to the occasion—the fear of the decline of social stability—by arguing that state support of religion is not necessary to the civil authority. Clustered about that central claim are the other prudential and cautionary points to be addressed to the Christian communities which hoped to profit from the law. Points 6-7 and again 9-11 display the bill as internally and externally deleterious to Christianity in particular.

By contrast, Points 1-4 and again Points 13-15 have a wider, more encompassing matter: humanity in general. The first asserts a positive theological

---

12. To display the bare bones of the argumentation I have stripped it of Madison's diction and added connectives.
    1. Because of the unconditional priority of religious duties over civil obligations, religion is wholly exempt from any secular direction.
    2. So much more so is it exempt from governmental interference.
    3. Therefore even the smallest infringement of religious liberty constitutes an insupportable breach.
    4. Governmental aid to religion is necessarily discriminatory and therefore violates the basic principle of equality.
    5. Furthermore it constitutes officials the judges of orthodoxy and enables them to use religion politically.
    6. At the same time it weakens Christianity by making it depend on secular support.
    7. Moreover, such aid contaminates the purity of Christianity.
    8. Above all, it is unnecessary to the security of a free government; indeed it is dangerous.
    9. It discourages immigration by signalling possible persecution.
    10. And it encourages emigration of dissenting citizens.
    11. It encourages violent animosity among the sects.
    12. In thus hindering free movement it in fact restricts the spread of Christianity.
    13. The attempt to enforce so unpopular a law will undermine social stability.
    14. Therefore before the bill is enacted into law the will of the majority should be fairly ascertained and represented in the legislature.
    15. Ultimately, however, religious liberty being coequal with the other natural rights, the legislature has in any case no authority to abridge it, unless it is granted to have unlimited power to take away all rights.

principle—the absolute priority of man's relation to God over his social bonds —as the ground for the inalienable character of the right to religious freedom; the second deduces from the first the prohibition of legislative interference in religion. The third point draws the political principle of prompt resistance to civil interference out of the uncompromisably absolute separation of the realms, the fourth draws from the philosophical principle of human equality the political injunction against state support of religion.

The closing numbers cite the forms and practices of popular government which proceed from the foundations established in One through Four as they bear on the bill. Thirteen warns against unenforceable laws, Fourteen states the majoritarian principle, and the last point recalls the principle of limited government to the offending legislature. The rhetorical force of this structure will, I think, tell even on a reader who does not apprehend it explicitly.

# III. Rhetorical Analysis of the Text[13]

## Preamble

*To the Honorable the General Assembly of the Commonwealth of Virginia*
*A Memorial and Remonstrance—*
    *We the subscribers, citizens of the said Commonwealth, having taken into serious*

---

13. Since the texture of the Remonstrance will sometimes be best brought out by comparison with Madison's other writings on religious liberty, that dearest of his causes, a list of his chief expressions on the subject is subjoined. I want to observe here that while Madison's language soon acquires a certain canonical quality it never becomes formulaic. —Iteration does not wear away its warmth.

   1. 1773–1775. A series of youthful letters addressed to his friend from Princeton, William Bradford. These were written when Madison was in his early twenties and express in youthfully vigorous language his disgusted preoccupation with evidences of religious persecution in Orange County and in Virginia.

   2. 1776. His first small but important contribution as a lawmaker, his amendment of George Mason's draft of Article XVI for the Virginia Declaration of Rights. Also his own rejected version.

   3. 1785. The "Memorial and Remonstrance," his most extensive writing on the subject.

   4. 1788. A note on the value of a multiplicity of sects, meant for the Virginia Convention.

   5. 1789. An early version and the final form of the first article of the Federal Bill of Rights, the First Amendment.

   6. 1792. Essay "On Property," expressing a theory of rights, and particularly religious rights, as constituting personal property.

   7. 1811. Presidential Veto Message, against the incorporation of the Episcopal Church.

   8. 1811, 1813. Presidential Thanksgiving Messages, with caveats about publicly ordered prayer.

*consideration, a Bill printed by order of the last Session of General Assembly, entitled "A Bill establishing provisions for Teachers of the Christian Religion," and conceiving that the same if finally armed with the sanctions of a law, will be a dangerous abuse of power, are bound as faithful members of a free State to remonstrate against it, and to declare the reasons by which we are determined. We remonstrate against the said Bill.*

The preamble alludes to the postponement resolution which had requested the people of the counties "to signify their opinion respecting the adoption of such a Bill"—the resolution is quoted in the next to last paragraph. The petition, then a common political instrument, is intended to elicit popular opinion in the course of lawmaking. Such moments of communication between the people and their representatives are an important part of Madison's theory of self-government, set out in the penultimate paragraph of the petition.

Not Madison but "We ... the citizens" speak. His style could well accommodate itself to a canonical anonymity. He had been trained in a school of rhetoric which eschewed idiosyncracies, and he never engaged in the luxuriously indignant periodicity peculiar to Jefferson.

This petition is presented in the form of a *remonstrance*, that is, a protest, a protest, suggestively, of the "faithful," but it is not a mere protest, as are most present-day petitions. It is also a *memorial*, a declaration of reasons—every paragraph begins with a "because"—in the tradition of the Declaration of Independence.

## First Paragraph

*1. Because we hold it for a fundamental and undeniable truth, "that Religion or the duty which we owe to our Creator and the manner of discharging it, can be directed only by reason and conviction, not by force or violence." The religion then of every man must be left to the conviction and conscience of every man; it is the right of every man to exercise it as*

---

9.  1819–1822. Letters demonstrating that state support is not necessary to the religious sects.
10. 1823. Letter to Edward Everett, on the secular university.
11. "Detached Memoranda" (fragmentary essays separated from his main works in the nineteenth century), containing historical notes and exhortations concerning religious liberty, and an account of the events around the Remonstrance.
12. 1832. A late letter to the Rev. Jasper Adams giving proofs from American history that Christianity is not in need of state support. The sources for these texts are 1. *Papers*, Vol. 1 (1751–1779), pp. 100–161 *passim*; 2. *ibid.*, p. 174; 3. *ibid.* Vol 8, pp. 298–304; 4. James Madison, *The Forging of American Federalism*, Saul K. Padover, ed. (New York 1965), p. 306; 5. Stokes, p. 345; 6. *ibid.*, p. 551; 7. *Forging*, p. 307; 8. Adrienne Koch, *Madison's "Advice to My County"* (Princeton 1966), pp. 33–34; 9. *Forging*, pp. 308–10; 10. Stokes, p. 348; 11. *op. cit.*, pp. 554–62; 12. *The Writings of James Madison*, Gaillard Hunt, ed., Vol IX, 1819–1836, (New York 1910) pp. 484–88.

*these may dictate. This right is in its nature an unalienable right. It is unalienable, because the opinions of men, depending only on the evidence contemplated by their own minds, cannot follow the dictates of other men: It is unalienable also, because what is here a right towards men, is a duty towards the Creator. It is the duty of every man to render the Creator such homage and such only as he believes to be acceptable to him. This duty is precedent, both in order of time and in degree of obligation to the claims of Civil Society. Before any man can be considered as a member of Civil Society, he must be considered as a subject of the Governor of the Universe: And if a member of Civil Society, who enters into any subordinate Association, must always do it with a reservation of his duty to the General Authority; much more must every man who becomes a member of any particular Civil Society, do it with a saving of his allegiance to the Universal Sovereign. We maintain therefore that in matters of Religion, no man's right is abridged by the institution of Civil Society and that Religion is wholly exempt from its cognizance. True it is, that no other rule exists, by which any question which may divide a Society, can be ultimately determined, but the will of the majority; but it is also true that the majority may trespass on the rights of the minority.*

The first is the most philosophical and the most rhetorically artful paragraph.

Madison begins by reminding the legislature of its own fundamental law; he quotes, as he notes in the margin of his copy, from Article XVI of the "Declaration of Rights and Frame of Government of Virginia," adopted in 1776. Madison himself intervened crucially in George Mason's draft of that article, though not in the clause here cited. (The sentence he affected is given in the fourth and fifteenth paragraphs.) In accordance with the symmetrical structure of the petition the Virginia Declaration is cited in the first, the fourth, the eleventh, and the fifteenth paragraphs.

The quotation from Article XVI is here introduced in the spirit of the Declaration of Independence—the Virginia Declaration has no such language—as an axiom, an undeniable truth. The consequences of that axiom are then developed in an enchained sequence of sentences which has something of the quality of a liturgical responsion, a kind of rondel of reason. The enchaining brings with it a non-periodic style. (A period, speaking technically, is a circuitlike sentence, whose meaning is not delivered until the whole is complete.) Several sentences are grammatically simple; conjunctions and relatives, regarded in school rhetoric as weakening the vivacity of writing since their function should be carried by the diction,[14] are avoided; the continuity indeed comes from the incantation-like diction.

"The religion of every man must be left to the conviction and conscience of

14. George Campbell, *The Philosophy of Rhetoric* (1776), Lloyd F. Blitzer, ed. (Carbondale, 1963), p. 365.

every man": he restates the phrase "reason and conviction" of Article XVI alliteratively and tactfully, avoiding the everlasting dwelling on the reason by which some of the defenders of religious liberty had made themselves suspect.

The recurrent phrase "every man," rather than "all men" as in the Declaration of Independence, carries a subtle emphasis: as Madison's logic notes from college point out, when one turns "all" into "every," the predicate is logically distributed so that it "belongs to every individual."[15] Since religion consists of "voluntary acts of individuals singly and voluntarily associated," Madison's use of "every" rather than "all" conveys the *individual* nature of religion implied by the fundamental axiom: no religious dogma is to be imposed and no religious exercise interfered with—the First Amendment in germ.

Each key word is picked up and elaborated as the argument continues: " ... it is the *right* of every man to exercise" religion freely. "This *right* is ... an *unalienable right*. It is *unalienable* also, because what is here a *right* toward men, is a *duty* towards the *Creator*. It is the *duty* of every man to render the *Creator* such homage" as seems right to him. "This *duty* is precedent ... to the claims of *Civil Society*." "Before a man can be considered a member of *Civil Society* ...," etc.

The rhetorical form emphasizes the mutual involvement of the terms. Free exercise of religion is a right and moreover an inalienable right because of an ineradicable feature of human nature—its freedom. This human freedom, the ground of civil liberty, is understood as a bondage of the mind to the dictates of reason and evidence—a dependency clearly expressed in the original opening paragraph of Jefferson's bill on religious freedom, which was deleted by the General Assembly with Madison's reluctant acquiescence:

Well aware that the opinions and beliefs of men depend not on their own will, but follow involuntarily the evidence proposed to their minds ...[16]

Madison, who had earlier displayed a lively interest in the philosophical question of mental liberty and misgivings about its possibility,[17] must indeed have been sorry to see this pertinent passage disappear from the bill, bartered away for its passage.

The right to religious liberty is inalienable because of man's nature, but also because of man's relation to God, which is that of a subject bound by a duty to his

---

15. *Papers*; Vol. 1, p. 38.
16. Frank Swancara, *Thomas Jefferson vs. Religious Oppression* (New York 1969), p. 124.
17. Samuel Stanhope Smith sent him a disquisition "on that knotty question of liberty and necessity," for light on which Madison had "frequently attacked" him. Madison's response is lost, but Smith observes in a later letter: "I have read over your *theoretical* objections against the doctrine of moral liberty; for *practically* you seem to be one of its disciples." (*Papers*, Vol. I, 1751–1779, pp. 194, 253). For Madison's theory of human nature in general see Ralph L. Ketcham, "James Madison and the Nature of Man," *Journal of the History of Ideas*, Vol. XIX, (1958), pp. 62–76.

Creator. Religion as defined in the passage from the Declaration of Rights which Madison quotes is a conflation of the Roman notion of obligatory performance and the biblical idea of obedience to the Creator, with the Christian salvational sense, to be introduced in the middle paragraphs, here missing.

The inalienability of the right is, then, rooted in man's nature as free and as created; it is therefore inalienable by the very reason which makes it a right, namely that it is a *divine* duty that must be *individually* discharged. Succinctly put: "What is here a right towards men, is a duty towards the Creator."

Now comes the crux of the paragraph and indeed of the work. Man's relation as a creature is prior both in time and in degree to his membership in a polity. Before he can be thought of as a citizen of civil society, he must be considered as a subject under the Governor of the Universe; as the former he has rights, as the latter duties. This priority in time may mean that these duties were his before this or any polity was instituted, even in the Garden of Eden, or that they precede adult citizenship and obligate even children. Precedent in "degree of obligation" must mean that moral duties supersede political obedience and that religion governs citizenship—indeed a creed for citizen-resisters to the usurpations of the civil powers.

Although Madison himself later cites Jesus' "own declaration that his Kingdom was not of this world" in behalf of the separation of worlds,[18] his own remarkable theory is quite distinct from the scriptural doctrine of the two realms, the secular and the spiritual. That doctrine holds this world inferior—Roger Williams, for example, demands a hedge between the *garden* of the Church and the *wilderness* of the World.[19]

In contrast the precedence of the religious realm set out in the Remonstrance is not seen from the perspective of the world beyond, but from the position of a practicing citizen of *this* world, albeit with prior obligations. That is precisely why the functionaries of civil society may not invade the realm of religion —because that realm is here conceived as belonging to the active life of the world, not to civil society but certainly to society. The suspicion and contempt of the world, on the other hand, against whose intrusions the soul and the church must be guarded, belongs to *Christian* liberty— a *theological condition* and not a *civil right*. (The defense of religious liberty from the scriptural point of view is rousingly made in Milton's *Treatise of Civil Power in Ecclesiastical Causes;* Madison may have known it.)

Madison is proposing a civil theology[20] in which the political arena is circumscribed by religion. From the point of view of political theory men come

18. "Detached Memoranda," p. 556.
19. Wilber G. Katz and Harold P. Southerland, "Religious Pluralism and the Supreme Court," *Religion in America, op. cit.*, p. 273.
20. Alexander Landi, "Madison's Political Theory," *The Political Science Reviewer*, Vol. VI (Fall 1976), pp. 77–79.

out of (though in a sense they never leave) the Lockean state of nature and its right to self-preservation; from the point of view of the civil theology man first and last remains "a free-born subject under the crown of heaven owing homage to none but God himself."[21]

Madison, however, does not advocate the cause of a deistic super-sect with its positive rationalistic doctrines, so confidently set out in Jefferson's bill concerning religious freedom which knows and approves "the plan of the holy author of our religion ... to extend it by the influence of reason alone." Encompassing all religions, whether propagated by reason, revelation, or force of tradition, Madison's civil theology is a genuine grounding for religious pluralism.

The conclusion is that rights of conscience are reserved from the authority of the political power. As Jefferson puts it in Query XVII of the *Notes on the State of Virginia* (1781):

Our rulers can have authority over such natural rights only as we have submitted them. The rights of conscience we never submitted, we could not submit. We are answerable for them to our God.

There follows an intricately wrought analogy containing more subtleties than bear articulating:

As 1. a member of Civil Society 2. who enters into any subordinate Association 3. must always do it 4. with a reservation of his duty 5. to the General Authority,

Much more so must 1. every man 2. who becomes a member of any particular Civil Society 3. do it 4. with a saving of his allegiance 5. to the Universal Sovereign.

The climax of the deduction from the axiom of religion as a duty to God is the radical proposition that "no man's right is abridged by the institution of Civil Society and Religion is wholly exempt from its cognizance." That is to say: 1. individual religious rights are not alienated upon entering civil society and 2. the realm of common religious observance is wholly out of its jurisdiction.

This is the seminal secular statement concerning religious liberty as a civil right in the public realm, since Jefferson's law, to which Madison later gave the honor of being the standard of expression on the subject, was, though prior in the drafting (1779), posterior in publication (1785).

The political consequences are reserved for the last paragraph of the petition. Madison, however, here adds an afterthought which brings these funda-

21. John Wise in *Vindication of the Government of New England Churches* (1717), quoted in Sidney E. Mead, "The 'Nation with the Soul of a Church'," *American Civil Religion*, Russell E. Richey and Donald G. Jones, eds. (New York 1974), pp. 53 ff.

mental principles into the political arena. It is an antithesis acknowledging in capsule form the paradox of majoritarianism, a clash of truths in the world of action:[22] "True it is" that the will of the majority alone can settle divisive differences, "but it is also true" that the majority may try to infringe the rights of the minority. The penultimate paragraph will counterbalance this reservation by an expression of full faith in the majority as a last court of appeal in cases of infringements on liberty.

## Second Paragraph

*2. Because if Religion be exempt from the authority of the Society at large, still less can it be subject to that of the Legislative Body. The latter are but the creatures and viceregents of the former. Their jurisdiction is both derivative and limited: it is limited with regard to the co-ordinate departments, more necessarily is it limited with regard to the constituents. The preservation of a free Government requires not merely, that the metes and bounds which separate each department of power be invariably maintained; but more especially that neither of them be suffered to overleap the great Barrier which defends the rights of the people. The Rulers who are guilty of such an encroachment, exceed the commission from which they derive their authority, and are Tyrants. The People who submit to it are governed by laws made neither by themselves nor by an authority derived from them, and are slaves.*

Now the doctrines of the first paragraph are applied, *a fortiori*, to government: if religion is beyond the political community, so much the more is it beyond the legislature. For as human beings are God's creatures, so the legislature is civil society's creature. (The manner of this legislative subordination is again taken up in the corresponding next to last paragraph.) The double limitation on its jurisdiction is stated in a succinct presentation of the theories of checks and balances and of limited government. It displays Madison's genius for articulating a full complement of fine but fundamental distinctions in the smallest compass: he speaks of the "metes and bounds" (a phrase possibly adapted from Locke's *Letter Concerning Toleration*[23]) that contain the departments of government, and of the "great Barrier" that circumscribes government itself.

That barrier, the limitation of legislative jurisdiction, is the political palisade before the "wall of separation," in Jefferson's famous metaphor for the First Amendment, which is to be erected between church and state.[24]

22. On Madison's views of the problems of majoritarian rule, see above all Federalist, no. 10; also Landi, pp. 84 ff.
23. See *Papers*, Vol. 8, p. 297.
24. See Jefferson's Letter to the Danbury Baptists, 1802; On Roger Williams. see Loren P. Beth, *The American Theory of Church and State* (Gainesville 1958), p. 65. The American author of the separation doctrine was Roger Williams, with whose ideas Madison was probably acquainted through his connection with the Baptists of his county.

The language of the following sentences grows terse and absolute (although Madison manages to tuck in definitions of both tyranny and slavery): the rulers who encroach are tyrants, the people that submits, slaves. The theory of prompt resistance to be set out in the next paragraph is prepared.

## Third Paragraph

*3. Because it is proper to take alarm at the first experiment on our liberties. We hold this prudent jealousy to be the first duty of Citizens, and one of the noblest characteristics of the late Revolution. The free men of America did not wait till usurped power had strengthened itself by exercise, and entangled the question in precedents. They saw all the consequences in the principle, and they avoided the consequences by denying the principle. We revere this lesson too much soon to forget it. Who does not see that the same authority which can establish Christianity, in exclusion of all other Religions, may establish with the same ease any particular sect of Christians, in exclusion of all other Sects? that the same authority which can force a citizen to contribute three pence only of his property for the support of any one establishment, may force him to conform to any other establishment in all cases whatsoever?*

The first sentence is often quoted, and "viewing with alarm" has, of course, become a cant phrase of American rhetoric. Here the key word "liberties" first appears; the phrase "religious liberty" is missing from the work.

The Revolution is invoked in favor of a "noble" mode of political response. In the remarkable phrase "prudent jealousy" Madison conflates republican duty with the principle of honor, the citizen's calculation of consequences with the nobleman's propensity for quick offense.

The necessity for a ready response lies, of course, in the fact that absolute principles, not compromisable interests, are involved; "the least interference with religion would be a flagrant usurpation." The Revolution being the complex event of both principle and interest, was in fact slow in coming:

... mankind are more disposed to suffer, while evils are sufferable, than to right themselves by abolishing the forms to which they are accustomed. (Declaration of Independence.)

Nevertheless Madison here propagates the view, for the sake of the "revered lesson" it contains, that the three-penny tax on tea moved "the free men of America" to revolt because it was a first signal of oppression, not the last straw.[25] This view was evidently dear to him, for later he wrote:

---

25. John Adams' entry in his Diary shows how the Boston Tea Party caught the imagination as a beginning: "This is the most magnificent Movement of all. There is a Dignity, a Majesty, a Sublimity, in this last Effort of the Patriots, that I greatly admire ... I can't but consider it as an Epoch in History." (December 17, 1773).

The people of the U.S. owe their Independence and their liberty, to the wisdom of descrying in the minute tax of 3 pence on tea, the magnitude of the evil comprized in the precedent.[26]

The lesson he urges is immediate recognition of and resistance to breaches of principle, and especially of the principle of religious liberty, because it stands and falls as a whole. As Locke says: "The civil power can either change everything in religion, ... or it can change nothing."[27]

Two balanced rhetorical questions next address first the churches and then the individual citizens: as the authority to establish Christianity implies the power to establish one sect, so the authority to touch a citizen's property implies the power to force him into religious conformity. This passage reveals Madison's universal view of religious liberty. He writes here, in hopeful suppression of the fact admitted in the eleventh paragraph, that Virginia still had a Christian establishment, as if the establishment were an incipient event to be feared by the sects. His vigorous promotion of Jefferson's bill concerning religious liberty shows that he knew otherwise. An episode that occurred during its consideration in the Assembly shows where his sentiments lay.

For the sake of passage Madison acquiesced in several deletions urged by men who objected to the aggressively deistic tone of the bill, although he thought these defaced the text somewhat—to him its expressions were ever the "true standard of religious liberty," even if his own inclination was to phrase that liberty as a right to the "full and free exercise" of religion rather than to its non-exercise. What he refused to agree to was an insertion that was attempted; as Madison much later recalled it:

... an experiment was made on the reverence entertained for the name and sanctity of the Saviour, by proposing to insert the words "Jesus Christ" after the words "our lord" in the preamble.[28]

Madison, ever vigilant of words, fought the insertion and it was dropped. On January 22, 1786, he reported to Jefferson in Paris in a spirit of modest triumph that the enacting clauses had passed without alteration and, "I flatter myself, have in this country extinguished forever the ambitious hope of making laws for the human mind." The rejection of the insertion proved, Jefferson later said, that "the Jew and the Gentile, the Christian and Mohametan, the Hindoo and Infidel of every denomination" were within the mantle of its protection. Those were exactly Madison's intentions, and indeed he was to receive expressions of gratitude from American Jews and to give encouragement to them.[29]

26. "Detached Memoranda," p. 557.
27. John Locke, *The Second Treatise of Government and A Letter Concerning Toleration*, J. W. Gough, ed. (Oxford 1976), p. 149.
28. Swancara, pp. 123–32; "Detached Memoranda," p. 556.
29. To Mordecai M. Noah, 1818; to Jacob de la Motta, 1820.

So, although in the Remonstrance he writes to and for and—unemphatically but unquestionably—as a Christian, there can be no question about the universal application of his principle of religious liberty. No more can there be doubt about his uncompromising steadfastness in its application. Of many proofs let me choose only three.

His early drafts of those amendments to the Constitution which were to become the Bill of Rights specifically prohibit the establishment of a "national religion."

Even in later life he retained his rhetorical vigor in fighting Christian establishments. He apostrophises his country:

> Ye states of America, which retain ... any aberration from the sacred principle of religious liberty, by giving to Caesar what belongs to God or joining together what God has put asunder, hasten to revise and purify your systems....[30]

As ever, he attacks the perverse wedlock of church and state on the ground of Christianity itself.

The most striking, almost comical, examples of his scrupulous avoidance of even the slightest trespass are his presidential Thanksgiving Messages during the War of 1812. Forced from him by a Congressional resolution, he phrased them rather as exhortations to free choice of worship than to public piety.[31]

The strong Madisonian meaning of the word "liberty" as applied to religion, to be adumbrated throughout the petition, begins to emerge: Religious liberty is a civil right which is grounded in relations of duty to God antecedent to political society and therefore incapable of being abrogated. These relations are determined by the nature of the human conscience which is free in a philosophical sense, that is, determined not by external force but only by the internal compulsion of evidence, be it reason or revelation; they are also determined by the original nature of the human being which is dependent in a theological sense, that is, created by God. (Para. 1.) Delicate because it must be maintained absolutely (Para. 3), this liberty requires the government to abstain completely from interference, either for the purpose of supporting or of obstructing the exercise of religious obligations (Para. 2). The government must protect religion, but only by abstaining evenhandedly from interference and by safeguarding each sect from the intrusions of the other sects (Para. 8). As a right held on the same political terms as the other natural rights which are reserved to the individual, religious liberty stands or falls with them (Para. 15).

30. "Detached Memoranda," p. 555.
31. Koch p. 33; cf. "Detached Memoranda." pp. 560–61.

## Fourth Paragraph

*4. Because the Bill violates that equality which ought to be the basis of every law, and which is more indispensible, in proportion as the validity or expediency of any law is more liable to be impeached. If "all men are by nature equally free and independent," all men are to be considered as entering into Society on equal conditions; as relinquishing no more, and therefore retaining no less, one than another, of their natural rights. Above all are they to be considered as retaining an "equal title to the free exercise of Religion according to the dictates of Conscience." Whilst we assert for ourselves a freedom to embrace, to profess and to observe the Religion which we believe to be of divine origin, we cannot deny an equal freedom to those whose minds have not yet yielded to the evidence which has convinced us. If this freedom be abused, it is an offence against God, not against man: To God, therefore, not to man, must an account of it be rendered. As the Bill violates equality by subjecting some to peculiar burdens, so it violates the same principle, by granting to others peculiar exemptions. Are the Quakers and Menonists the only sects who think a compulsive support of their Religions unnecessary and unwarrantable? Can their piety alone be entrusted with the care of public worship? Ought their Religions to be endowed above all others with extraordinary privileges by which proselytes may be enticed from all others? We think too favorably of the justice and good sense of these denominations to believe that they either covet pre-eminences over their fellow citizens or that they will be seduced by them from the common opposition to the measure.*

The proposed bill violates the natural equality of men affirmed in Article I of the Virginia Declaration of Rights, now quoted by Madison. Such equality is presented here as an *internal* condition of all law. The more liable a law is to the charge of invalidity or inexpediency, the more important such equality becomes. The dictum that equality "ought to be the basis of every law" refers to the inner equity of the law, which ought to affect everyone equally, not to the familiar demand for equality of treatment under the law; the law must be such as to be *capable* of equal application.

A succinct statement of the contract theory of rights which underlies this demand is given: All men being by nature equally free, they must enter civil society on equal conditions; they must give up and retain exactly equal rights. "To embrace, to profess, and to observe the Religion which we believe to be of divine origin," to join, to declare, and to exercise whatever religion seems to us to be truly a religion, is the essence of these rights with respect to religion.

In the conclusion of his *Letter Concerning Toleration* Locke says that "the sum of all we drive at is that every man may enjoy the same rights that are guaranteed to others." Madison italicizes this one word in the petition—*equal*—when he quotes for the first time that clause of Article XVI of the Virginia Declaration of Rights for whose form he himself was responsible. Equality of application was for Madison, as for Locke, important above all else. Although it intends to preserve the "liberal principle" of Article XVI, by "abolishing all distinctions of pre-eminence" among the different sects, the Assessment bill is inequitable because it burdens all in support of a religious service that will peculiarly burden non-Christians and peculiarly exempt those Christians who do not wish to take advantage of its benefits. The rhetorical question what sects besides those mentioned would fall under the latter category would have the obvious answer: above all the Baptists, whose opposition to any kind of state intervention was a matter of theological principle.

There can never be a moral or theological pretext for interference, because the abuse of the right of religion is not subject to human punishment. Madison had restricted Mason's broad reservation in the original draft of Article XVI, that the magistrate might restrain free exercise if, "under colour of religion, any man disturb the peace, the happiness, or the safety of society" to the condition that "the preservation of liberty and the existence of the State are manifestly endangered." His record shows that as a magistrate he would have found no occasion to apply it; presumably he was glad finally to see the whole clause drop out.[32]

A bilaterally symmetrical sentence, the only one in the petition to contain the word "God," presents this central point.

Early American documents mention the names of God profusely enough to intrigue a medieval theologian.[33] In this petition he is the Creator to whom man owes the duties of a dependent creature; the Governor of the Universe to whom man is a subject rather than a citizen (Para. 1); God before whom alone man can sin (Para. 4); the Author of our Religion who hands down its teachings in scripture (Para. 6); the Supreme Lawgiver of the Universe from whom illumination of the legislature is requested (Para. 15). Not mere unreflective Enlightenment epithets, these names must be genuine expressions of Madison's understanding of the facets of humanity's relations to God, for they delineate just such a God as would be the ground of religious liberty.

In his work on Article XVI of the Declaration of Rights,[34] the young delegate to the Revolutionary Convention of May 1776 had offered but one draft article, on religion. Patrick Henry, who had himself sponsored it, had quickly disclaimed it when challenged on the floor to explain whether he actually intended to disestablish the Church. Madison had, of course, intended just such disestablishment:

That Religion or the duty we owe to our Creator, and the manner of discharging

32. *Papers*, Vol. 1, pp. 172–75.
33. For example, in the Declaration of Independence there is "Nature's God," man's "Creator," "the Supreme Judge of the World." In his law Jefferson used one designation that pleased the devout, "holy author of our religion," the very one employed by the Baptists in their resolution against the assessment bill (James, p. 138).
34. See *Papers, op. cit.* pp. 170 ff.

it, being under the direction of reason and conviction only, not of violence or compulsion [a stylistic emendation of Mason's "force or violence"], all men are equally entitled to the full and free exercise of it according to the dictates of Conscience ...

No man or class of men, the article continues, should receive special privileges or be subjected to special penalties for religious reasons, a prefiguration of the two prongs of the First Amendment, the establishment and free exercise clauses.

Madison, having been forced to withdraw his own draft, scrutinized Mason's version, which promised "the fullest *toleration* in the Exercise of religion." He alone, perhaps, in that assembly took one word of it seriously enough to forestall a danger.[35]

That word was "toleration," which implies not a right to religious liberty but a privilege granted. That was absolutely insufferable for Madison, for toleration accorded with, and so confirmed, ecclesiastical establishment (as in modern times it can accompany an anti-clerical policy).[36]

Although he wrote respectfully of the Dutch "experiment of combining liberal toleration with the establishment of a particular creed,"[37] Madison would certainly have rejected Spinoza's views in the *Theologico-Political Treatise* (Ch. XIX), that the possessor of sovereign power has rights over spiritual matters but should *grant* religious liberty on matters of outward observancy, only inward piety being private and inalienable. In any case, it is unlikely that he knew Spinoza's writings, especially since Locke, whose *Letter* he had probably read (as external likelihood and internal evidence in the Remonstrance indicate), admitted to little acquaintance with Spinoza's work.[38] Although called a "Letter Concerning Toleration," Locke's work, by a typical cunning twist, shifts the meaning of the term: not *granted* to dissenting Christians by the ecclesiastical establishment and its state sponsors, toleration is *required* of the magistrate toward all churches —Mohametan, Pagan, idolaters (though not—and here Madison differed—to atheists); the magistrate has no right to interfere with either the internal or the external aspects of religion. This "tolerance" was not the notion Tom Paine excoriated in the *Age of Reason* as "not the *opposite* of Intolerance, but ... the *counterfeit* of it," but a demand for a right under cover of a less aggressive term. Madison might well have taken his lead from the thought of the *Letter Concerning Toleration* at the same time that he balked at the use of the term "toleration" in fundamental law.

---

35. See Hunt, "James Madison and Religious Liberty," *op. cit.* p. 166.
36. Stokes, pp. 22–26.
37. Letter to Edward Livingston, 1822; to Rev. Adams, 1832.
38. Locke started writing on toleration in the decade before Spinoza's *Treatise*, which appeared in 1670, though the *Letter* postdated it (1683–4). For Locke's lack of interest in Spinoza see Leo Strauss, *Natural Right and History* (Chicago 1974), p. 211.

## Fifth Paragraph

*5. Because the Bill implies either that the Civil Magistrate is a competent Judge of Religious Truth; or that he may employ Religion as an engine of Civil policy. The first is an arrogant pretension falsified by the contradictory opinions of Rulers in all ages, and throughout the world: the second an unhallowed perversion of the means of salvation.*

This brief but resounding paragraph ("arrogant pretension"—"unhallowed perversion") appears to have been retained from the debate on the floor of the Assembly. Madison's notes show that he employed his large theological erudition[39] to bring home to the Assembly, with that muted irony of which he was capable, the politico-theological consequences of the bill. It would require a legislative definition of Christianity: it would require that the lawmakers choose an official Bible—Hebrew, Septuagint, or Vulgate, decide the method of its interpretation, confirm a doctrine—Trinitarian, Arian, Socinian—as orthodox, and so forth. The sentiment of the paragraph is Lockean: "neither the right nor the art of ruling does necessarily carry along with it the certain knowledge of other things and least of all of the true religion."

In this paragraph alone Madison speaks of religion as a "means of salvation," in contrast to its employment as an "engine of civil policy." In the argument for religious liberty the obligations of religion, not its blessings, count most.

## Sixth Paragraph

*6. Because the establishment proposed by the Bill is not requisite for the support of the Christian Religion. To say that it is, is a contradiction to the Christian Religion itself, for every page of it disavows a dependence on the powers of this world: it is a contradiction to fact; for it is known that this Religion both existed and flourished, not only without the support of human laws, but in spite of every opposition from them, and not only during the period of miraculous aid, but long after it had been left to its own evidence and the ordinary care of Providence. Nay, it is a contradiction in terms; for a Religion not invented by human policy, must have pre-existed and been supported, before it was established by human policy. It is moreover to weaken in those who profess this Religion a pious confidence in its innate excellence and the patronage of its Author; and to foster in those who still reject it, a suspicion that its friends are too conscious of its fallacies to trust it to its own merits.*

Madison leaves the universal considerations of religious liberty to attend to the particularly Christian interest in it. The seven core paragraphs of the petition are devoted to that Christian point of view, an arrangement that tellingly mirrors

---

39. See, for example, the theological catalogue for the library of the University of Virginia which he hastily tossed off at Jefferson's urgent request, listing an astonishing number of church writers of the first five Christian centuries. (Rives, pp. 641–44).

both the encompassing necessity for a philosophical foundation and the immediate fact that a Christian constituency is speaking. Establishment, prohibited in a purely political context for the sake of the free exercise of religion, is to be yet more eschewed for the sake of Christianity itself.

His notes for the floor debate show that he intended to divert the argument from the preoccupation with the social need for religion to the "true question": Are religious establishments necessary for religion? The proponents' concern with "the peace of society" were, so he implies later, in part a cover for concern with the declining importance of the churches. The end of war, laws that cherish virtue, religious associations which would provide personal examples of morality, the education of youth, and precisely the end of governmental intrusion, not state intervention, were the "true remedies" for the decline of religion which he recommended to the legislature.[40]

Madison's Christian defense of liberty is in the great tradition of Protestant dissenting writings, especially Milton's *Treatise of Civil Power in Ecclesiastical Causes* (1659), in which he shows "the wrong the civil power doth; by violating the fundamental privilege of the Gospel ... Christian libertie,"[41] that is, freedom from forcible impositions in matters of worship. Indeed Milton's whole argument is drawn from scripture, especially from the Pauline letters.

Madison, too, alludes to scripture: "every page" of religion "disavows a dependence on the power of this world." The Baptists, whose whole petition was based on the grounds that the bill was "repugnant to the Spirit of the Gospel," however, outdid him in this line of argument. For them, as for other opposing Christians, disestablishment dated literally from Jesus himself. "Render to Caesar the things that are Caesar's, and to God the things that are God's" (*Mark* 13, 17).

The paragraph next exposes the contradictions of the bill's premise that Christianity cannot be diffused "without a competent provision" for its teachers. The contradiction of *fact* is that Christianity has indeed flourished at all times without aid—and Madison gives a believer's capsule history of its two epochs, the era of miracles and the era of ordinary providence. The more serious contradiction in *terms* is twofold: the dependence of religion, which is pre-existent, on human policy and the failure of the faithful to trust in God for its support. The argument is rendered in beautifully branching and balanced cola.

Fifty years later, Madison would feel entitled to answer the "true question" definitively from the accumulated evidence of the American experience, which had "brought the subject to a fair and finally decisive test." Left to itself,

---

40. Landi, pp. 80–84.
41. John Milton, *Selected Prose*, C. A. Patrides, ed. (Penguin 1974), p. 316.

religion would flourish; indeed the danger lay rather in its extravagances.[42] Madison insisted that "every successful example of a perfect separation ... is of importance," and that he regarded such success as an indispensable empirical test of the principle of religious liberty. At the same time, he was certain that the test would never fail since "there appears to be in the nature of man what insures his belief in an invisible cause...." But what would Madison have said in the face of an observable decline of "religious commitment"?[43]

## Seventh Paragraph

7. *Because experience witnesseth that ecclesiastical establishments, instead of maintaining the purity and efficacy of Religion, have had a contrary operation. During almost fifteen centuries has the legal establishment of Christianity been on trial. What have been its fruits? More or less in all places, pride and indolence in the Clergy, ignorance and servility in the laity, in both, superstition, bigotry and persecution. Enquire of the Teachers of Christianity for the ages in which it appeared in its greatest lustre; those of every sect, point to the ages prior to its incorporation with Civil policy. Propose a restoration of this primitive State in which its Teachers depended on the voluntary rewards of their flocks, many of them predict its downfall. On which Side ought their testimony to have greatest weight, when for or when against their interest?*

Proof positive that religion could flourish on its own was a half-century in the future, but the evidence of fifteen centuries, that is, dating back roughly to the Conversion of Constantine, showed that legal establishments corrupted Christianity, because they hampered freedom of conscience, "the truly Christian principle."[44]

Here, as elsewhere, Madison allows himself the most spirited language for clerical degeneracy, without, however, giving way to that automatic anti-clericalism that possessed Jefferson. Even in his youth, in an early letter to his friend William Bradford (Jan., 1774), he had given a similar catalogue of clerical and lay vice, of the "Pride ignorance and Knavery among the Priesthood and Vice and Wickedness among the Laity," evident in his home country; worst of all:

---

42. Letter to Rev. Jasper Adams, 1832. The opinion here expressed seems to have been current. For example, just the preceding year Tocqueville had asked a Catholic priest whom he had met in his travels through the Michigan Territory this very question: "Do you think that the support of the civil power is useful to religion?" —and had received the same answer Madison was to give to Rev. Adams, a decided negative. See George Wilson Pierson, *Tocqueville in America*, Dudley C. Lunt, ed. (Gloucester 1969), p. 203.

43. Evidence for such a long term decline in the second half of this century is given in Rodney Stark and Charles Y. Glock, *American Piety: The Nature of Religious Commitment*, Vol. 1 (Berkeley 1970) pp. 204 ff. Of course, the question would become moot, should a massive religious revival refute the sociological projections.

44. "Detached Memoranda", p. 554.

That diabolical Hell conceived principle of persecution rages among some and to their eternal Infamy the Clergy can furnish their Quota of Imps for such business.

The Protestant supporters of the bill would preach the life of early Christianity, but they do not want to live like the first disciples, much less like the first Teacher himself. This passage deals with church business without resorting to the word "church," which never occurs in this petition. Madison opposed not only the "incorporation with Civil policy" effected by a bill proposing state-salaried religious teachers, but the "encroachments and accumulations" encouraged by the legal incorporation of churches.[45] He desired neither state-supported nor richly endowed churches, but small congregations which would directly support their ministers.

## Eighth Paragraph

*8. Because the establishment in question is not necessary for the support of Civil Government. If it be urged as necessary for the support of Civil Government only as it is a means of supporting Religion, and it be not necessary for the latter purpose, it cannot be necessary for the former. If Religion be not within the cognizance of Civil Government how can its legal establishment be necessary to Civil Government? What influence in fact have ecclesiastical establishments had on Civil Society? In some instances they have been seen to erect a spiritual tyranny on the ruins of the Civil authority; in many instances they have been seen upholding the thrones of political tyranny; in no instance have they been seen the guardians of the liberties of the people. Rulers who wished to subvert the public liberty, may have found an established Clergy convenient auxiliaries. A just Government instituted to secure & perpetuate it needs them not. Such a Government will be best supported by protecting every Citizen in the enjoyment of his Religion with the same equal hand which protects his person and his property; by neither invading the equal rights of any Sect, nor suffering any Sect to invade those of another.*

At the middle count, Madison takes up the main point supposedly agitating the proponents of the bill: the dangerous decline of morality which the bill was supposed to halt.

In his very first extant expression concerning religious liberty, a youthful letter to Bradford (Dec., 1773), Madison had asked this politico-theological question: "Is an Ecclesiastical Establishment absolutely necessary to support civil society in a supream Government?"

In this petition Madison has prepared the ground for answering the question in such a way that he can dispose of it by a mere syllogism (*modus tollens*): Only if religion is within the cognizance of government can the question of necessary legal establishment arise. But it is not, by the first

45. "Detached Memoranda," p. 556–57.

paragraph. Therefore establishment is not necessary. With equal logic, he disposes of the circular arguments of the supporters, who say that establishment is necessary to government only insofar as government is a necessary means of supporting religion; since the latter contention has been shown false by the preceding paragraph, the former falls also.

So logical a resolution of the great question was not universally appealing. After he heard these arguments, Henry Lee wrote to Madison: "Refiners may weave as fine a web of reason as they please, but the experience of all times shows Religion to be the guardian of morals." Not really in disagreement with Lee's premise, Madison only disclaimed the inference that government ought to support the churches; he certainly never went as far as Jefferson, who claimed that "the interests of society require observation of those moral precepts only on which all religions agree,"[46] which amounts to saying that any church is unnecessary to society.

There are some instances of establishments supplanting governments, many instances of their upholding tyrannies, none of their supporting liberty. "A just government, instituted to secure and perpetuate it, needs them not," concludes Madison, in the language reminiscent of the Declaration of Independence: "That to secure these Rights, Governments are instituted among Men, deriving their just Powers from the Consent of the Governed."

How does a just government protect religious rights? It protects them precisely as it protects property and other rights. In a short essay "On Property,"[47] written in 1792, Madison elaborates a remarkable theory of religious rights which goes further: Rights are property: "In a word, as a man is said to have a right to his property, he may be equally be said to have a property in his rights ..." And earlier in the same essay: "He has a property of peculiar value in his religious opinions, and in the profession and practice dictated by them ..." Just government is instituted to secure property, in the large sense in which the term includes anything which a person values as his own (leaving to everyone else a like advantage), of which dominion over external things is only a part. Religious rights so conceived establish a kind of internal personal, and external sectarian, territoriality which government is to protect by "neither invading the equal rights of any Sect, nor suffering any Sect to invade those of another."

---

46. Beth, p. 66. Madison's own church allegiance was so vanishingly weak a factor in his opinions about religious liberty that it can be relegated to a footnote. He was, in fact, a born Episcopalian with strong Presbyterian associations from his Princeton days, apparently a communicant of no church, who displayed unfailing respect for the faiths of the sects.
47. Stokes, p. 551. The starting point of the essay appears to be Locke's definition of property as life, liberty and estate in the *Second Treatise of Government*, Ch. IX.

## Ninth and Tenth Paragraphs

*9. Because the proposed establishment is a departure from that generous policy, which, offering an Asylum to the persecuted and oppressed of every Nation and Religion, promised a lustre to our country, and an accession to the number of its citizens. What a melancholy mark is the Bill of sudden degeneracy? Instead of holding forth an Asylum to the persecuted, it is itself a signal of persecution. It degrades from the equal rank of Citizens all those whose opinions in Religion do not bend to those of the Legislative authority. Distant as it may be in its present form from the Inquisition, it differs from it only in degree. The one is the first step, the other the last in the career of intolerance. The magnanimous sufferer under this cruel scourge in foreign Regions, must view the Bill as a Beacon on our Coast, warning him to seek some other haven, where liberty and philanthrophy in their due extent, may offer a more certain repose from his Troubles.*

*10. Because it will have a like tendency to banish our Citizens. The allurements presented by other situations are every day thinning their number. To superadd a fresh motive to emigration by revoking the liberty which they now enjoy, would be the same species of folly which has dishonoured and depopulated flourishing kingdoms.*

Now Madison inserts two complementary considerations, humanitarian and practical, which had figured in the floor debates under the heading of "Policy." The bill might close Virginia as a religious asylum and also drive out dissenters, and might thus at once prevent much-needed immigration and further thin a population already moving westward at an alarming rate. Madison did not have to spell out to his fellow farmers the bad economic results of this policy: a yet greater shortage of labor power and further declining land prices.

The politically regressive consequences, however, needed telling. Citing again his maxim of the contiguity of the least and the greatest breach of liberty, he does not hesitate to compare, though with reasonable qualifications, a Protestant Establishment with the Catholic Inquisition.

The springiness of style that derives from the adroit use of the two dictions of English, the long latinate and the short Anglo-Saxon, is noteworthy; for example: "What a *melancholy mark* is the Bill of *sudden degeneracy?*"

## Eleventh Paragraph

*11. Because it will destroy that moderation and harmony which the forbearance of our laws to intermeddle with Religion has produced among its several sects. Torrents of blood have been spilt in the old world, by vain attempts of the secular arm, to extinguish Religious discord, by proscribing all difference in Religious opinion. Time has at length revealed the true remedy. Every relaxation of narrow and rigorous policy, whereever it has been tried, has been found to assuage the disease. The American Theatre has exhibited proofs that equal and compleat liberty, if it does not wholly eradicate it, sufficiently destroys its malignant influence on the health and prosperity of the State. If with the salutary effects of this system under our own eyes, we begin to contract the bounds of Religious freedom, we know no name that will too severely reproach our folly. At least let warning be taken at the first fruits of the threatened innovation. The very appearance of the Bill has transformed "that Christian forbearance, love and charity," which of late mutually prevailed, into animosities and jealousies, which may not soon be appeased. What mischiefs may not be dreaded, should this enemy to the public quiet be armed with the force of a law?*

A crowd of notions familiar in early American rhetoric is now brought to bear on the threat of sectarian strife raised by the bill: Time has revealed, and America is the stage to test and prove, the remedies to old problems; liberty once instituted, innovations may be dangerously regressive.

The paragraph permits itself some hyperbole, in the claim of complete religious freedom in Virginia, which flies in the face of the fact that the same Article XVI which Madison cites establishes Christianity, if not as a state church, at least as the public morality; moreover, in 1781 Jefferson had indignantly noted that although "statutory oppression" had ceased, common law permitting all sorts of persecution was still on the books.[48]

In this section Madison prudently suppresses his opinion that a vigorous variety of sects is an even more practically efficacious guarantee of liberty than a bill of rights,[49] and that disestablishment promotes church prosperity very much as factions well managed produce political stability. The unstated premise is, of course, that doctrinal enthusiasms are as much an irrepressible force of human nature as special secular interests.

I can detect no strain in this opinion of Madison which might equate it with the insouciant dogma that truth is a private predilection and that everything is "true for" them that believe it. His preference for sectarian variety rests on the limits and necessities of observed human nature, not on a doctrinal disavowal of the search for truth.

## Twelfth Paragraph

*12. Because the policy of the Bill is adverse to the diffusion of the light of Christianity. The first wish of those who enjoy this precious gift ought to be that it may be imparted to the whole race of mankind. Compare the number of those who have as yet*

---

48. *Notes on the State of Virginia*, Query XVII.
49. Madison liked to quote Voltaire's Article on "Tolerance" in the *Philosophical Dictionary*: "If one religion only were allowed in England, the government would possibly become arbitrary; if there were but two, the people would cut each other's throats; but as there are such a multitude, they all live happy and in peace." See Koch, p. 76.

*received it with the number still remaining under the dominion of false Religions; and how small is the former! Does the policy of the Bill tend to lessen the disproportion? No; it at once discourages those who are strangers to the light of revelation from coming into the Region of it; and countenances by example the nations who continue in darkness, in shutting out those who might convey it to them. Instead of Levelling as far as possible, every obstacle to the victorious progress of Truth, the Bill with an ignoble and unchristian timidity would circumscribe it with a wall of defence against the encroachments of error.*

In his notes for the floor debate Madison had proposed to himself at about this place in the argument a vindication of disestablished Christianity, a "panegyric of it on our side." He omits it in the Remonstrance in favor of an appeal to the missionary urge. The offending bill is altogether too parochially conceived. Not only in Virginia but throughout mankind should Christianity be propagated. Instead the bill will act to prevent conversions by discouraging "strangers to the light of revelation," that is, infidels, (Madison had first written "light of truth" and then christianized the term) from "coming into the Region of it," which implies that a free America ought to be the natural ground on which revealed religion may be experienced.

The final sentence of the Christian section is reminiscent of the great peroration of Jefferson's bill establishing religious freedom.

That truth is great and will prevail if left to herself: that she is the proper and sufficient antagonist to error and has nothing to fear from the conflict unless by human interposition disarmed of her natural weapons, free argument and debate,

except that the truth of this paragraph is truth of revelation, and the freedom here called for Christian liberty, a very Madisonian harmonizing of the spirit of enlightenment and the claims of Christianity.

## Thirteenth Paragraph

*13. Because attempts to enforce by legal sanctions, acts obnoxious to so great a proportion of Citizens, tend to enervate the laws in general, and to slacken the bands of Society. If it be difficult to execute any law which is not generally deemed necessary or salutary, what must be the case, where it is deemed invalid and dangerous? And what may be the effect of so striking an example of impotency in the Government, on its general authority?*

Again balanced phrases: "enervate the laws ... slacken the bands," "necessary or salutary ... invalid and dangerous." The rhetorical questions are intended to give pause to legislators who are ignoring the dangerous political effects of an unenforceable law: Madison's associates anticipated rebellion in some counties.

## Fourteenth Paragraph

*14. Because a measure of such singular magnitude and delicacy ought not to be imposed, without the clearest evidence that it is called for by a majority of citizens, and no satisfactory method is yet proposed by which the voice of the majority in this case may be determined, or its influence secured. "The people of the respective counties are indeed requested to signify their opinion respecting the adoption of the Bill to the next Session of Assembly." But the representation must be made equal, before the voice either of the Representatives or of the Counties will be that of the people. Our hope is that neither of the former will, after due consideration, espouse the dangerous principle of the Bill. Should the event disappoint us, it will still leave us in full confidence, that a fair appeal to the latter will reverse the sentence against our liberties.*

In accordance with the symmetry of the composition, the penultimate paragraph returns to the beginning. The resolution which occasioned the petition is cited, though with a little rhetorical interjection ("indeed") reflecting on its insufficiency.

Self-government, Madison argues, demands both that the voice of the majority be determined and that its influence be secured. That is to say, the legislature's occasional solicitation of petitions is not a methodical enough polling of opinion, and electoral qualifications as well as legislative apportionment are not fair enough for either the Delegates or the Senators to be truly representative.[50] Truly representative representatives, namely those elected from districts fairly apportioned and responsive to their constituents, would have been less likely to support the dangerous abuse of power perpetrated by the bill. The petitioners hope, however, that even the legislature as presently constituted can be brought to reconsider its dangerous course. The paragraph concludes with a veiled threat of an organized grass-roots campaign for repeal should the bill nonetheless be passed.

Here is set out an important aspect of Madison's theory of self-government. It is the idea that when major and controversial legislation is in progress, the people should be given some systematic opportunity to express themselves, because such a plebiscitic element is a trustworthy preventive of legislative usurpation and an added sanction for laws. (There is, however, no evidence that Madison was proposing that this "method" for determining the voice of the majority be incorporated in the constitution.)

Accordingly, the fact that Jefferson's law on religious liberty had been overwhelmingly passed in the wake of this and other petitions was regarded by Madison as a consummating factor: it had the "advantage of having been the result of a formal appeal to the sense of the Community and a deliberate

---

50. Jefferson, too, had complained of the under-representation in both houses of the middle and upper counties, and of the arms-bearing population in general.

sanction of a vast Majority ..."[51] The majoritarian faith Madison expresses here is, of course, qualified in other contexts where he designs devices, "moderations of sovereignty," for protecting liberties from the people as well as from the legislature.

## Fifteenth Paragraph

*15. Because finally, "the equal right of every citizen to the free exercise of his Religion according to the dictates of conscience" is held by the same tenure with all our other rights. If we recur to its origin, it is equally the gift of nature; if we weigh its importance, it cannot be less dear to us; if we consult the "Declaration of those rights which pertain to the good people of Virginia, as the basis and foundation of Government," it is enumerated with equal solemnity, or rather studied emphasis. Either then, we must say, that the Will of the Legislature is the only measure of their authority; and that in the plenitude of this authority, they may sweep away all our fundamental rights; or, that they are bound to leave this particular right untouched and sacred: Either we must say, that they may controul the freedom of the press, may abolish the Trial by Jury, may swallow up the Executive and Judiciary Powers of the State; nay that they may despoil us of our very right of suffrage, and erect themselves into an independent and hereditary Assembly or, we must say, that they have no authority to enact into law the Bill under consideration. We the Subscribers say, that the General Assembly of the Commonwealth have no such authority: And that no effort may be omitted on our part against so dangerous an usurpation, we oppose to it, this remonstrance; earnestly praying, as we are in duty bound, that the Supreme Lawgiver of the Universe, by illuminating those to whom it is addressed, may on the one hand, turn their Councils from every act which would affront his holy prerogative, or violate the trust committed to them: and on the other, guide them into every measure which may be worthy of his [blessing, may re] dound to their own praise, and may establish more firmly the liberties, the prosperity and the happiness of the Commonwealth.*

The right of religious liberty is now examined not insofar as it is grounded in transpolitical conditions, as in the opening paragraph, but with respect to its situation in the political realm. Madison again quotes his free exercise clause of Article XVI, as he evidently had in the floor debates, together with a sonorous adaptation of the full title of the Virginia Declaration of Rights:

"A declaration of rights made by the representatives of the good people of Virginia, assembled in full and free convention; which rights do pertain to them and their posterity, as the basis and foundation of government."

The purpose of the citation in the fourth paragraph was to emphasize the equal *application* of the right; the point now is the equal, or even superior,

---

51. "Detached Memoranda," p. 554.

*standing* that it has compared with the other fundamental rights. The religious right is equal with them in its natural origin, in its importance, and in its place of promulgation in fundamental law. (It had in fact been given the ultimate, most emphatic, position, even beyond the article of exhortation to virtue and "frequent recurrency to fundamental principles.")

Since it is coequal with the other fundamental rights, religious liberty stands or falls with them. The argument, presented in two parallel sets of alternatives, recurs to the all or nothing reasoning of the third paragraph which is now extended: The least breach of the religious right endangers all the rights at once: Either the will of the legislature is unlimited or this particular right is untouchable; either they may sweep away all rights or they cannot enact the present bill. All the phrases are precise and suggestive: "Will of the legislature" is opposed to "voice of the people" of the previous paragraph; the "plenitude of their authority" conveys legislative high-handedness; "sacred" is used in the double sense of holy and inviolable. The rights of which the legislature "may despoil us"—Madison had first written "may abolish" but then remembered that natural rights cannot be abolished—are then enumerated from the Declaration, but their order is almost exactly reversed, ending with the most specifically political right, a "fundamental article in Republican Constitutions," the right of suffrage.[52] The whole appeal is couched in terms of the constraints of reasonable speech: "Either we must say ... or we must say ..." It concludes determinedly: "We the Subscribers say, that the General Assembly of this Commonwealth have no such authority."

The final pronouncement of the citizens, then, supersedes all the previous considerations. It is the principled denial of legislative authority to enact the bill at all.—The legislators may not arm it "with the sanctions of a law," in the words of the preamble. Into the last paragraph of his law concerning religious freedom Jefferson had written just such a denial: No assembly can constrain a future one equally elected by the people, but it is free to shame it by declaring that if it should repeal or narrow the law, "such an act will be an infringement of natural right."

The subscribers' pronouncement introduces the submission of the Remonstrance in a peroration which counters the simplicity of the opening with a grand, intricately branching rhetorical period, praying, as religious duty demands, that two coordinate illuminations might descend on the law-makers, that they may both refrain from violating their trust, and pass measures which will make them worthy of God's blessing, will procure for them the praise of men, and will establish for the citizens liberty, prosperity, and happiness.

Observe the careful enumeration of goods in triads and subtriads; such triples belong to the familiar rhythms of American rhetoric: "Life, liberty, and

52. *Forging*, p. 36.

the pursuit of Happiness" rise most immediately to the ear. The prayer for the *establishment* of these goods echoes Jefferson's title: "A Bill for Establishing Religious Freedom," which proclaims the republican appropriation of the offending term. The petition ends as it began, with a reference to the Commonwealth.

# IV. Madison's Rhetoric

How is the rhetoric of the Remonstrance to be characterized and how is it to be accounted for, reticent and rousing, calculated to persuade and designed for truth-telling, concisely compendious and artfully structured, as it is?

In his essay "Of Eloquence," Hume complains of the deficiency of modern eloquence. It is "calm, elegant, and subtle," but also lacking in passion and sublimity as well as order and method: it is mere "good sense delivered in proper expressions." The Remonstrance has the precise virtues and precisely lacks the shortcomings Hume names. It is at once "argumentative and rational," grandly passionate and carefully constructed. It is almost as if Madison had composed to Hume's standards, standards probably more appropriate to written than to spoken eloquence.—Unlike Jefferson, whose style failed him on the floor, Madison, incidentally, was a persuasive though undeclamatory speaker. He seems to have addressed assemblies with just the same educated elegance with which he wrote, suiting his matter rather than his form to the occasion.

The terms and criteria for judging style used to be fairly fixed; they were to be found in textbooks of rhetoric, or—the preferred word in the eighteenth century—of eloquence, and they were universally employed in characterizing and judging productions. The loss of such a set critical vocabulary is not much mourned by modern writers on rhetoric who regard it as meaningless and unprofitable, and demand more fluid, sophisticated criteria. But its disappearance *is* a loss. To be sure, a writer was unlikely to improve his style through learning Quintilian's maxim that the first virtue of eloquence is perspicuity or clarity, that vivacity or liveliness of imagery is next in order of importance, that elegance or dignity of manner is also required, and that the intellect has the prerogative of being always the faculty ultimately addressed in speech. (My source here is Campbell's *Philosophy of Rhetoric*, 1776, a work based mainly on Humean principles of human nature and popular as a textbook in the colleges of the early Republic.[53]) Yet it seems to me a suggestive fact that in the era when

53. Campbell, *The Philosophy of Rhetoric, op. cit.*, pp. 215–16, 285, 35. I. A. Richards, for example, in his *Philosophy of Rhetoric* (New York 1965), p. 70, decries the use of just such terms as "misleading and unprofitable."

these criteria were considered significant, prose was produced which indeed satisfied them. Certainly they describe Madison's style with accuracy.

They were, I suppose, not so much the instigators as the precipitates of a well-defined and uncompromising taste—well-defined insofar as a deviation truly offended, and uncompromising because no one, certainly not Madison, lowered his language for any audience or occasion. All the manifestos, pamphlets, correspondences, petitions, memoranda, and memorials of the time that come in one's way show the same educated correctness of style.

Such correctness, then called purity, that is, speech true to its rules, is said by Campbell to be the lowest—and indispensable—rhetorical virtue: "Where grammar ends, eloquence begins." It was in such basic studies that Madison, and everyone of his class, was amply trained, and that early, in boyhood.

At twelve, Madison recalls in his Autobiography, he was learning Greek and Latin, studies which, if not absolutely indispensable to good style, at least insure that knowledge of syntax and vocabulary which prevents illogical constructions and faulty diction, while shaping the latinate English appropriate to the political writing; "Miscellaneous literature" was also embraced by the plan of the school he attended. Madison devotes a special paragraph to one such work of literature which he read early to great advantage, namely the *Spectator*, especially Addison's numbers, and in recommending it late in life to his nephew, he writes:

Addison was of the first rank among the fine writers of the age, and has given a definition of what he showed himself to be an example, 'Fine writing,' he says, 'consists of sentiments that are natural, without being obvious'; to which adding the remark of Swift, another celebrated author of the same period, making a good style to consist 'of proper words in their proper places,' a definition is formed, which will merit your recollection ...[54]

Madison has here conjoined precepts from one writer of satiny sweetness and another of mordant savor. Both together evidently guided his taste.

The young student apparently had an interest in rhetorical lore; at one point he copied out and annotated a long poem on the tropes of rhetoric:

A metaphor compares with out the Sign [Madison's marginalia: "as, like, etc."]
Virtue's A star and shall for ever shine.[55]

Studies conducive to good style and rational discourse continued in Princeton. There he filled a copybook with notes on a course of logic, probably given by the president, Dr. Witherspoon, much of which naturally bore on

54. Rives, p. 25, n. 1. It is the spirit of Swift's definitions which I. A. Richards' rhetoric is intended to oppose.
55. *Papers*, Vol. 1, pp. 32–42.

argumentation.[56] There, too, he is very likely to have heard Dr. Witherspoon's lectures on eloquence, of which extensive notes taken, among others, by Madison's college friend William Bradford in 1772, are still extant.[57] Witherspoon was fully conscious that he was speaking to young men destined for political responsibilities, who might one day have to address "promiscuous assemblies." He tried to convey to them the dignity and efficacy of rhetorical studies. He deals with the usual topics: types of language, such as the sublime and the simple; the use of tropes or figures of speech; his own set of characteristics for eloquent writing—for example it is just if it pays "particular attention to the truth and meaning of every sentence" and elegant if it employs "the best expression the language will afford." Furthermore he treats of invention, organization, and style, always giving examples, and among them Addison and Swift.

But what seems to me most likely to have penetrated to his young auditors was his introductory list of five rules for good writing: 1. "Study to imitate the greatest examples." 2. "Accustom yourselves to early and much composition and exercise in speaking." 3. Acquaint yourselves with the "branches subordinate" to eloquence, namely grammar, orthography, punctuation. 4. Notice and guard against "peculiar phrases," namely idiosyncracies of speech. 5. "Follow nature," meaning, gain clear conceptions and follow the truth. Who now is bold enough to give such good advice so authoritatively?

Rives thought that Witherspoon had had a major part in forming Madison's style. Both show

the same lucid order, the same precision and comprehensiveness combined, the same persuasive majesty of truth and conviction clothed in a terse and felicitous diction,

words which surely describe Madison's style faithfully. —Evidently good style, if not great eloquence, can be taught.

One far from negligible feature of this early training was the prodigious amount of studying Madison—and Jefferson as well—did in their youth. Madison reports that he lost his health and nearly his life at Princeton through all too successfully cramming two year's work into one. But as a result both men were masters of their style early: Jefferson was thirty-three when he wrote the Declaration and Madison composed the Remonstrance at thirty-four. Yet these efforts, being completely self-imposed, never spoiled the savor of study for either man. Madison went to his books throughout his life; for example, no sooner had he been appointed deputy of the Constitutional Convention than "he turned his attention and researches to the sources ancient and modern of

56. *Papers*, Vol. 1, pp. 18–19.
57. Microfilm, Princeton University Library.

information and guidance as to its object. Of the result of these he had the use both in the Convention and afterwards in the 'Federalist'." And later, at the close of his public life, he devoted himself to his farm and his books.[58] Such continuous, ready recourse to reading both for private pleasure and political practice is surely a chief contributor to fluent expression.

But of course, the most minute history of his studies is as insufficient to account for Madison's eloquence as the most time-honored rubrics of eloquence are to describe it. Finally, it seems to me, his rhetoric is shaped by that rare aptitude for conjoining speech and action, which caused Jefferson in his own Autobiography to couple in his noble description of Madison "the powers and polish of his pen, and the wisdom of his administration." That capacity was part of a

> habit of self-possession which placed at his ready command the rich resources
> of his luminous and discriminating mind ... Never wandering from his subject
> in vain declamation, but pursuing it closely in language pure, classical, and
> copious, soothing always the feeling of his adversaries by civilities and softness
> of expression ... With these consummate powers were united a pure and
> spotless virtue which no calumny has ever attempted to sully.

In the traditional understanding the rhetorical art has three parts: first, and least, elements of style such as copious diction and felicitous syntax; next, devices of persuasion such as "civilities," prudent omissions and emphases together with well-placed passion; and finally, the very conditions of good speech, the veracity of the speaker and the verity of his thought. By these criteria, Madison was a consummate rhetorician.

* * *

Madison's "Memorial and Remonstrance" seems to me in truth among the finest of those works of republican rhetoric in which adroit enunciation of the principles of liberty elicits their practice. In particular, that strict separation of church and state which implies the total secularization of public life and which, when promoted with heedless or rabid rationalism causes me, at least, some unease, is set forth in the Remonstrance with such respectful, even reverent, reasonableness that my scruples are dissolved in a certain enthusiasm for Madison's principles and in the gratitude that a Jew and a refugee must feel for the safe haven he made.

And yet the question obtrudes itself whether such texts, for all their

---

58. "James Madison's Autobiography," Douglas Adair, ed., *William and Mary Quarterly*, Third Series, II, no. 2, pp. 202, 207. See also Robert A. Rutland, "Madison's Bookish Habits," *The Quarterly Journal of the Library of Congress*, Vol. 37, no. 2 (Spring 1980), pp. 176–91.

fineness, are not relics of an irrecoverable art. A document to whose phrases the highest court of the land has recourse in formulating decisions affecting every school in every district of the country can, of course, hardly be relegated to history. Nonetheless, it is perhaps no longer a possible model of public discourse. I ask myself why that might be.

I can imagine four reasons which would be readily forthcoming. It will be said that the public will no longer listen to educated speech, and it will be said that politicians can no longer be expected to have the requisite training. And again, it will be claimed that the level of language itself has fallen, and also that the complexity of our condition precludes any grandly perspicuous statement of principles.

These may be true reasons, but they are also bad excuses. They merit indignant refutation as miserable collusions with mere or imaginary circumstance. How we will be spoken to, how we and our representatives will be educated, to what level the language will rise, how our thought will dispose the world—these matters are not yet in the hands of Society or the Historical Situation, but in ours. And in the exercise of the liberties in which that truth is realized Madison is not only a possible, but the best possible, model.

# APPENDIX

## The Remonstrance in Supreme Court Decisions

The after-history of the petition is chiefly that of its citation by the Supreme Court.[59] The Court has recurred to the Remonstrance for elucidation of the "establishment" clause of the First Amendment, both because the latter was also drafted by Madison and because the Remonstrance is concerned with religion in education, as are so many cases involving that clause.

The relevant part of the First Amendment runs:

Congress shall make no laws respecting an establishment of religion, or prohibiting the free exercise thereof.

It includes two clauses, one prohibiting aid, and the other obstruction, to religion. That is to say, the "establishment" clause prohibits official support of

---

59. Sources: Irving Brant, *The Bill of Rights, Its Origin and Meaning* (New York 1967), pp. 400–18; *The Supreme Court and Education*, Classics in Education No. 4, David Fellman, ed. (New York 1976), Pt. 1, pp. 3–124.

religious institutions, while the "free exercise" clause guarantees absence of coercive invasions of any individual's religious practice. (Justice Clark, 1963). In this country, happily, the court has to deal far more often with putative attempts at establishment than with more direct interference with the free exercise of religion. Therefore the question of the precise meaning of the term "establishment" remains continually acute.

Madison's wording of the establishment clause is not vague but extremely careful, careful, that is, to use the most encompassing language. Thus the phrase "a law respecting" an establishment conveys a wider notion than would have been contained in the briefer phrase "a law establishing" religion, and, as Justice Rutledge points out, an "establishment of religion" is a wider notion than would have been an "establishment of a church." Such observations, however, are only the beginning of an interpretation; the central matter is the recovery of Madison's meaning of the word "establishment" itself, and here the Remonstrance, which was composed to combat an establishment of religion, is naturally the most pertinent document.

The Remonstrance played its chief role in the *Everson* decision of 1947. Everson, as a district taxpayer in New Jersey, filed a suit challenging a statute authorizing local Boards of Education to reimburse parents of parochial school students equally with parents of public school students for money expended on bus transportation. The argument was that such state aid to religious education constituted an establishment of religion under the First Amendment as made applicable to the states by the Fourteenth. Although the Court held that this particular statute did not constitute such an establishment, Justice Black in the course of his opinion paraphrased the Remonstrance at the climax of his argument for a very strong interpretation of the First Amendment:

The "establishment of religion" clause of the First Amendment means at least this: Neither a state nor the Federal Government can set up a church. Neither can pass laws which aid one religion, aid all religions, or prefer one religion over another.

Justice Rutledge canvassed the Remonstrance at yet greater length for his dissent, to find in it that broad meaning of the word "establishment" which would be consonant with the evident breadth of language of the First Amendment just pointed out. He found the word to have a wider scope of application than that current in England, where it usually meant a state church established by law.[60] Establishment, he showed, could encompass measures of all sorts and degrees, including, above all, state aid to any activity associated with religion,

60. Stokes, pp. 26–30, gives a history of the term. The contemporary political use of the phrase "The Establishment" is, of course, quite different since it has no reference to legal confirmation.

especially when coming out of tax money. He argued that all such government support whatsoever was vigorously proscribed under the name of establishment by the Remonstrance and hence by the First Amendment. Therefore the New Jersey statute supporting the children's way to parochial schools was unconstitutional. Rutledge thought the Remonstrance so fundamental a document that he appended it to his dissent.

In short, the justices who have cited the Remonstrance have almost all understood it as enjoining an absolute separation of church and state, and have construed the First Amendment accordingly—a construction named by a Jeffersonian phrase the "wall of separation" doctrine. Justice Frankfurter cites the Remonstrance once again in 1948, in the *McCollum* opinion, finding unconstitutional the device of so-called "released time," which permitted religious groups to come into public schools to instruct children who were released from the classroom for that purpose. He alone, incidentally, had an ear for that note of the document which could hardly get full hearing in a judicial context: its "deep religious feeling." Again, in 1963 Justice Clark quotes from the third paragraph, that "it is proper to take alarm at the first experiment on our liberties," to support prohibition of even minor incursions of the state into religion, such as the reading of a super-sectarian prayer in school.

But this agreement on intent has not been sufficient to decide cases. The Remonstrance has several times been used on both sides, as in the *Everson* case and, much earlier, in the Mormon marriage case of 1879. There Justice Waite endorsed its doctrine that religion was not within the cognizance of the government, but found nevertheless that it did not protect religious practices made criminal under the law of the land, such as polygamy. Madison himself had confessed "that it may not be easy, in every possible case, to trace the line of separation between the rights of religion and the Civil authority,"[61] though he thought that the doubts would arise on inessential points. In other words, like all fundamental documents, the Remonstrance is necessary but not sufficient for determining cases.

It should be noted that the one judge who wished to give the Remonstrance and Madison's views a narrowly historical interpretation, Justice Reed in his *McCollum* dissent, cites as traditionally permissible involvement of the government in religious affairs the existence of chaplains of Congress and of the armed forces—evidently unaware that Madison had most emphatically opposed the first and only tolerated the latter.[62] (Such toleration is rationalized by present day courts under the category of "neutralizing" aids, breaches of the wall of separation permitted to counterbalance restrictions on the free exercise of religion incidental to meeting governmental demands, such as service in the

61. Letter to Rev. Jasper Adams, 1832.
62. "Detached Memoranda," pp. 558–60; Letter to Edward Livingston, 1822.

armed forces.) Madison, however, excused such practices only reluctantly by the aphorism "the law ignores trifles."[63]

Furthermore the judge who rejected most forcefully "a too literal quest for the advice of the Founding Fathers" (Brennan, 1963), largely on the grounds that conditions of education have changed, failed to recall that the two new issues he mentions, universal public schooling and religious diversity, were precisely among the chief preoccupations of both Jefferson and Madison.

It is as hard to find fault with the strong interpretation of the First Amendment in the light of the Remonstrance as it is to deny the principles themselves of the Remonstrance. Yet one must wonder whether, were Madison alive now, he would not recognize certain complicating circumstances, especially where education is concerned.

Within the context of the Constitution the establishment clause is essentially ancillary to the free exercise clause. —It is because state aid to religion inevitably in some way restricts someone's free exercise that it is prohibited. Furthermore, the Court has repeatedly held that irreligion, secularism, humanism are all entitled to protection under the First Amendment, that is to say, they are in some manner of speaking religions, "belief systems": "the day that the country ceases to be free for irreligion it will cease to be free for religion ..." (Justice Jackson, *Zorach v. Clauson*, 1952). Consequently there is, by the Court's own admission, a sense in which secular schools are not neutral in respect to religious doctrine.

Might not Madison, the fairest of men in such arguments,[64] have honored the point, if moderately made, that the enormous preemption of a child's time for secular purposes implied by modern school-attendance requirements, considered together with the financial hardship which Justice Rutledge admits the policy of total separation imposes on parents wishing to give their children religious schooling, amounts to a state invasion of religious rights? Would he not have lent an attentive ear to the admission made by Justice Black (*Epperson v. Arkansas*, 1968) that nonreligious schooling cannot help but be, as for example in the teaching of evolution, in some sense anti-religious, and that the mandated secularism[65] of the public schools is indeed in the sense before explained, a kind of religious establishment, possibly in need of counterbalancing by fairly vigorous "neutralizing aids?" To study Madison's writings on religious liberty is to conceive an ardent wish that he might be here to consider these dilemmas.

---

63. *Religion in America*, William C. Mclaughlin and Robert N. Bellah (Boston 1968), p. 275; "Detached Memoranda," p. 559.
64. An example is his reply to Rev. Adams, 1832.
65. For the definition of secularism, see Stokes, pp. 30–31. Just this year [1980] the secular religion issue has again been raised in *Seagraves vs. State of California*.

# 2

# JUDICIAL RHETORIC

## WALTER BERNS

It is not clear that there is a proper place for rhetoric in the judiciary, even at the highest level of the judiciary, and especially when the judiciary is reviewing the constitutionality of legislation. The duty of the judges, Hamilton says in the 78th *Federalist*, is to defend or preserve the Constitution; they are to be its "faithful guardians." They stand not as did Horatius at the gates of Rome and armed with a sword; they sit in a courtroom and hear arguments made in cases or controversies, and they are armed only with their judgment.

Here is an example—albeit a hypothetical example—of a case over which the federal courts have jurisdiction. The state of Texas, having lost patience with the federal government's dilatory tactics for dealing with Castro's Cuba, and citing the many injuries and indignities suffered at the hands of Cuban officials, grants a commission to John Connally authorizing him to fit out armed vessels and, with them, to seize Cuban commerce. The Justice Department, hearing of this, rushes to a federal court asking for an injunction, and the case is joined. To decide it, the court looks to the Constitution for guidance; in a sense, it looks to the Constitution for its major premise and finds it in these words of Article I, section 10: "No state shall ... grant Letters of Marque and Reprisal...." Exercising its judgment where, alone, judgment is needed—namely, in the establishment of the minor premise—it determines that the commission granted to John Connally is a letter of marque and reprisal. The conclusion then follows as conclusions must. Rhetoric plays no part in this case or, specifically, in the opinion announcing the decision.

Rhetoric, as we learn from Aristotle, is the faculty of finding the means of persuading an audience, including a courtroom audience; but Aristotle's references to forensic rhetoric have mostly to do with persuading a jury of the guilt or innocence of a defendant, and I presume this conference is not interested in that. It could be interested in the rhetoric, if such it be, employed by counsel in the effort to persuade the judges. But persuade them of what? There is no doubt concerning first principles (or major premises); they are set down in the Constitution. Aristotle puts it this way: "As to whether a thing is important or unimportant, just or unjust, the judge must surely refuse to take his instructions from the litigants: he must decide for himself all such points as the law-giver has not already defined for himself."[1] And in the case I have given you, what is left undefined? Who can doubt that the commission given John Connally is a letter of marque and reprisal? It fits exactly the law dictionary definition of one. In truth, it is modelled on that definition; it had to be modelled on it rather than on an actual case because in the almost 200 years of its existence the federal judiciary has never had cause to decide such a case. The Supreme Court alone has decided thousands of constitutional cases, but never one involving letters of marque and reprisal, and seldom, if ever, one so simply disposed of.

But even in the real, as opposed to the hypothetical cases, it would appear that it would be improper for litigants, through their counsel, to employ rhetoric. "It is not right to pervert the judge by moving him to anger or envy or pity," says Aristotle; "one might as well warp a carpenter's rule before using it."[2] Sound advice, that; but is the Constitution so straight as a carpenter's rule, and are its standards so clear? Hamilton may have thought so, but he knew, nevertheless, that more than a deductive skill would be required of federal judges. They would also require "an uncommon portion of fortitude," he said in *Federalist* 78, on those occasions when "legislative invasions of [the Constitution] had been instigated by the major voice of the community." Carpentry does not require fortitude: judging—at least, American constitutional judging—requires an uncommon portion of it. This passage reminds us of something important: It is one thing to defend the Constitution against a potential tyrant, for example, or even against a state that decides to have its own foreign policy; but it is another thing to defend it against a popular majority. That majority will have to be addressed by the judges, and the only way it can be addressed effectively is rhetorically.

Madison knew this. His colleague, Jefferson, had proposed that "whenever any two of the three branches of government shall concur in opinion, each by the voice of two thirds of their whole number, that a convention is necessary for altering the Constitution, or *correcting breaches of it*, a convention shall be called for the purpose." Madison acknowledged such an arrangement to be, in principle, in accord with republican theory, but there were, he said, "insuperable objections" to it. One of these objections speaks to this question of judicial rhetoric:

...it may be considered as an objection inherent in the principle that as every appeal to the people would carry an implication of some defect in the government, frequent appeals would, in great measure, deprive the government of that

1. Aristotle, *Rhetoric*, 1354a28-1354b31.
2. Aristotle, *Rhetoric*, 1354a24-26.

veneration which time bestows on everything, and without which perhaps the wisest and freest governments would not possess the requisite stability. If it be true that all governments rest on opinion, it is no less true that the strength of opinion in each individual, and its practical influence on his conduct, depend much on the number which he supposes to have entertained the same opinion. The reason of man, like man himself, is timid and cautious when left alone, and acquires firmness and confidence in proportion to the number with which it is associated. When the examples which fortify opinion are ancient as well as numerous, they are known to have a double effect. In a nation of philosophers, this consideration ought to be disregarded. A reverence for the laws would be sufficiently inculcated by the voice of an enlightened reason. But a nation of philosophers is as little to be expected as the philosophical race of kings wished for by Plato. And in every other nation, the most rational government will not find it a superfluous advantage to have the prejudices of the community on its side.[3]

Later in the same paper, he complains that under Jefferson's arrangement, the passions of the public would sit in constitutional judgment, whereas "it is the reason, alone, of the public, that ought to control and regulate the government." In fact, however, Madison depends on the passions of the public.

Jefferson's proposal was not, of course, adopted; and, instead of *popular* review, we have *judicial* review. That, surely, was known by Madison to be the alternative. On the basis of this passage we can say that, in their role as faithful guardians, the judges must act to strengthen, or "fortify," the popular attachment to the Constitution, or, to cause it to be venerated by the people. They must come to revere it and, therefore, to be guided by it even when it might appear to be not in their interests to be so guided. Here is where judicial rhetoric must be employed. A "nation of philosophers" could be persuaded by deductive reasoning, but a nation of Americans can be persuaded only by appeals to the passions. Passion will come to the aid of reason, the reason that is embodied in the Constitution. The President may be said to employ rhetoric to reconcile the people's wants with the genuine needs of the country; the judges employ rhetoric to reconcile the people's wants with the institutions of republican government.

Our federal judges were quick to perform this function. Ralph Lerner has shown how, on circuit, the early Supreme Court justices used the occasion of the charge to grand juries to educate their less sophisticated countrymen in republican principles; to employ his words, the Court served as "Republican Schoolmaster."[4] And John Marshall employed rhetoric in the first great case to which his name is attached. The Court held in *Marbury* v. *Madison* that it did not have jurisdiction to decide the issue that Marbury brought, but Marshall, writing for the Court, reached that issue only after addressing himself to at least two others.

3. *Federalist* 49.
4. Ralph Lerner, "The Supreme Court as Republican Schoolmaster," in Philip B. Kurland (ed.), *The Supreme Court Review 1967* (Chicago: The University of Chicago Press, 1967), pp. 127-180.

He did this because he had something of importance to say to the President and Secretary of State and, most of all, to his as well as to every future generation of Americans. For example, he wanted to say that the "very essence of civil liberty certainly consists in the right of every individual to claim the protection of the laws, whenever he receives an injury."[5] It is no exaggeration to say that *Marbury* v. *Madison* was a rhetorical triumph: the institutional means of defending the Constitution against legislative and executive encroachments—judicial review— was established without cost to anyone other than William Marbury, and the price to him (the loss of an office that he could not have occupied anyway) was minimal if not nonexistent.

Marshall agreed with Hamilton that the chief function of the federal judiciary was to be faithful guardians of the Constitution. In one of his most celebrated opinions he said that we "must never forget that it is a constitution we are expounding."[6] How do the judges obey this admonition? Marshall himself was a very effective advocate of the Constitution during the Virginia ratification debates, but the arguments employed then might not serve so well now. Madison made this point in *Federalist* 49: "We are to recollect that all the existing constitutions were formed in the midst of a danger which repressed the passions most unfriendly to order and concord; of an enthusiastic confidence of the people in their patriotic leaders, which stifled the ordinary diversity of opinions on great national questions; of a universal ardor for new and opposite forms, produced by a universal resentment and indignation against the ancient government; and whilst no spirit of party connected with the changes to be made, or the abuses to be reformed, could mingle its leaven in the operation." So fortunate a combination of circumstances could not, he concluded, be expected in the future. (Within a few years Lincoln was to make the same point in a remarkably similar argument in a remarkably effective public speech.[7]) The "patriotic leaders" were able to discuss the issues dispassionately, but this cannot be said, or could not have been said, of the mass of the population. The debates in the Philadelphia convention are characterized by discussion on the level of principle (particularly in the period, before the adoption of the so-called Connecticut Compromise, during which they were debating the principle of representation), without descending to the level of interest. This can also be said of the debates in the first Congress over the Bill of Rights. These men knew, for example, the connection between church-state separation and toleration, and between toleration and the prevention or avoidance of tyranny; but the participants in the future debates, who will be concerned not with the form and principles of free government but, instead,

---

5. *Marbury* v. *Madison*, 1 Cranch 137, 163 (1803).
6. *MuCulloch* v. *Maryland*, 4 Wheat. 316, 407 (1819).
7. Abraham Lincoln, "The Perpetuation of Our Political Institutions: Address Before the Young Men's Lyceum of Springfield, Illinois, January 27, 1838," in Roy P. Basler (ed.), *Abraham Lincoln: His Speeches and Writings* (Cleveland and New York: The World Publishing Co.), pp. 83-4.

with a concrete political issue, will have interests to defend, interests to which they will be passionately attached. It is to these latter-day debaters (rather than to James Madison, the Federalist, and Melancton Smith, the Antifederalist) that the judiciary must speak. And how shall the judges speak? Even if they forever bear in mind Marshall's admonition, how do they obey it?

Not, surely, by writing disquisitions on toleration (to choose that example again), or by simply citing Locke's *Letters* on the subject. Locke could persuade Jefferson (who took copious notes on them, notes from which he then proceeded to draft the Virginia Bill for Establishing Religious Freedom), but Locke could not, I think, persuade the American Nazi Party or the Jews of Skokie, Illinois. The constitutional principles were established in a setting that was remarkably free of politics in the ordinary sense, but the setting in which the judiciary is called upon to defend and preserve them is characterized by politics in the ordinary sense. This is why the judges must be skillful political speakers.

How do the judges persuade the country, and especially the southern part of the country, that laws requiring black children to attend schools from which white children are excluded are violations of the Constitution? Indeed, are they violations of a principle on the basis of which this country was founded? In the event, the Court chose to rely on modern social science. Quoting from an *amicus* brief, the Court said that segregation with the sanction of law has the tendency to retard the educational and mental development of the black children. "Whatever may have been the extent of psychological knowledge at the time of *Plessy* v. *Ferguson* [the case in which the separate but equal principle was adopted], this finding is amply supported by modern authority."[8] But, as we know, and as the judges should have known, that finding was not supported by modern authority, and the enemies of the decision had a field day pointing this out. Modern authority ought to have had nothing to do with the decision; what was at stake was ancient, or at least venerable, principle, and the decision ought to have turned on the question of whether there were any reasons, as there sometimes are, why that principle should not be enforced.

I cite this case because it does represent a failure of judicial rhetoric and also because, by speaking of "modern authority," the justices provided me with a phrase that can serve as a metaphor of my complaints of the contemporary judiciary. Instead of defending constitutional principle from popular majorities, the Supreme Court especially has come to see its function as that of imposing "modern authority" on a population that is not disposed to accept it. What we have is not a case of the people versus the Constitution, but a case of some peculiar modern authorities versus the rest of us. The Constitution is being kept up to date, in tune with the times, as the Court's friends put it, and what they mean is, with the *New York Review of Books* by way of the New York *Times*. This is altogether improper.

8. *Brown* v. *Board of Education.* 347 U.S. 483, 494 (1954).

The point I must make here I have made before in the following passage:

> When the Court first decided that it was invested with the power to invalidate laws contrary to the Constitution, Marshall pointed to the fact that the Constitution requires the justices to take an oath to support it. Of course, other officers are also required to take an oath, and the Constitution even specifies the exact words of the oath required of the President; but Marshall said the oath applied "in an especial manner" to the judges. It is customary to dismiss this argument as carrying no weight whatever, but as Paul Eidelberg has pointed out, it is a mistake to do so. In an important respect, the judges' position is unique among the various officers of government—by which I mean, their relation to the Constitution is unique. Unlike other officers, judges have no constituents. Members of the House of Representatives are most unlike the judges in this respect, because some if not most of their authority comes from the people in their districts. They represent their people; but the judges, lacking living constituents, represent the Constitution and derive all their authority from it. As representatives of the Constitution, judges may have to listen to the representatives of the people, but it is not their office to represent the people, or to fancy themselves the interpreters and expositors of the will of living people; the Constitution provides other offices to do that. The judges should be disposed against change.[9]

It was not Marshall's view, or the Founders', that the Constitution must be kept in tune with the times, but, on the contrary, that the times, *to the extent possible*, be kept in tune with the Constitution. It is when we recognize the implications of that phrase "to the extent possible" that we come to appreciate the need for judicial rhetoric.

The people representing the times have to be persuaded to acknowledge that it is in their interest, their interest rightly understood, to be guided by the Constitution even if this means forgoing their immediately perceived interest, and this is not always readily or easily accomplished. In our day it is rarely even attempted. What the Court attempts, instead, is to persuade the people to accept judgments that derive not from the Constitution, but from these modern authorities. To do this, they have to depart or stray from the constitutional text, and, to the extent that they stray, their rhetorical task becomes even more difficult.

The reason for this can be readily grasped. As Aristotle says in the *Rhetoric*, "things that are true and things that are better are, by their nature, practically always easier to prove and easier to believe in."[10] And the American people, despite the efforts of a certain element in the intellectual community, continue to cling to the salutary and altogether reasonable idea that the Constitution embodies

9. Walter Berns, "The Least Dangerous Branch. But Only If . . .," in Leonard J. Theberge (ed.), *The Judiciary in a Democratic Society* (Lexington, Mass, and Toronto: Lexington Books, 1979), p. 12. Marshall's statement may be found in *Marbury* v. *Madison*, 1 Cranch 137, 180 (1803). The reference to Eidelberg is to his *The Philosophy of the American Constitution* (New York: The Free Press, 1968). p. 239.

10. Aristotle, *Rhetoric*, 1355a38-9.

the true principles of republican government. They seem to be more attached to the Constitution than are the judges and the intellectuals who constantly enjoin the judges to keep the Constitution "up to date" or "in tune with the times."[11] Whether this affection for the Constitution can survive the violating of its text is, however, questionable.

No decisions of the contemporary Court have been less popular, or, at least, have provoked greater anger or given rise to more determined opposition than the decision legalizing abortion on demand. A large part of the American people were not, and are not, persuaded that the judgments in those cases derive from the Constitution. And they are right. They derive from a right to privacy that the Court originally found not in the constitutional text or in any one of the amendments making up the Bill of Rights, but in "penumbras, formed by emanations from those [Bill of Rights] guarantees that help give them life and substance."[12] Which is to say that like the lovers who seek and need it, the right to privacy was found lurking in the shadows.

In this case, at least, the Court was forthright enough to be specific as to the provisions casting those shadows; they were the First, Third, Fourth, Fifth, Ninth, and Fourteenth Amendments, which, together, cast a shade large enough to hide anything the Court wanted to find. In the abortion cases, however, the Court found it unnecessary to specify where the right to privacy was to be found. It is there somewhere. "This right to privacy, whether it be founded in the Fourteenth Amendment's concept of personal liberty and restrictions on state action, as we feel it is, or, as the District Court determined, in the Ninth Amendment's reservation of rights to the people, is broad enough to encompass a woman's decision whether or not to terminate her pregnancy."[13] One place or the other, and like Iolanthe, the Court didn't care which. The important thing was to keep the Constitution in tune with the times, and the times were said to demand abortion on demand.

11. Whether this conservatism is a characteristic peculiar to the American people or is true of all people, I do not know. I do know that Locke drew important conclusions from what he said was true, namely, that the people "are not so easily got out of their old forms as some are apt to suggest." *Second Treatise of Civil Government*, sec. 223.

One reason for this attachment to the Constitution is implied in this complaint of Justice Frankfurter: "The tendency of focusing attention on constitutionality is to make constitutionality synonymous with wisdom, to regard a law as all right if it is constitutional." *West Virginia State Board of Education* v. *Barnette*, 319 U.S. 624, 670 (1943). Dissenting opinion.

It is a somewhat simpler matter to trace the idea that the Constitution should be kept up to date. No American jurist has been more celebrated in intellectual circles than Oliver Wendell Holmes, Jr., and it was Holmes who popularized the idea that the law should be in accord with "the felt necessities of the time." He said this of the common law, but he and his followers applied it to constitutional law, where its consequences have been pernicious. See Holmes, *The Common Law*. ed. Mark De Wolfe Howe (Cambridge: Harvard University Press, 1963). p. 5.

12. *Griswold* v. *Connecticut*, 381 U.S. 479, 484 (1965).

13. *Roe* v. *Wade*, 410 U.S. 113, 153 (1973).

It is no insignificant thing to declare void the laws of fifty states and the District of Columbia. One would think that the Court would hesitate even if these laws, like my fictitious letter of marque, clearly violated some express provision of the Constitution. And one would also think that the Court would make every effort to persuade us of the constitutional necessity to invalidate them. Nothing of the sort is to be found in the Court's opinion in *Roe* v. *Wade*, an opinion that covers fifty-one pages (one for every law declared unconstitutional) in the United States Reports.

I must make it clear that I am not here addressing myself to the issue of abortion as such; I am concerned with the Court's decision and, more specifically, its opinion supporting that decision. Were I required to decide whether mothers should be permitted, as a matter of their own convenience, to abort the child—or the foetus—they are carrying, I think I would have to address myself to the ontological question of whether an unborn child is a human being, a person and, as such, protected by the Constitution. Much as I might deplore having to consider questions of the family in terms of rights—the rights of the mother versus the rights of the father versus the rights of a child—or, in other words, much as I might deplore treating friends and lovers as legal adversaries (and I have written about this), since the Court has imposed this mode of analysis on me, I would feel obliged to consider whether that foetus has constitutional rights. (I might investigate those shadows in which the Court found the mother's right to privacy.) I might do this because I would feel obliged to do it. The Court did not.

Leaving aside the qualifications, the Court held that the Constitution forbids states to forbid abortions during the first six months of a pregnancy. The mother's constitutional right to privacy forbids states to do this. After the first six months, the mother's constitutional right may be made to give way—but not to any right of the foetus. That is, the Court does not hold that at seven months the foetus becomes a person with rights; it holds that at seven months there may be a compelling state interest in protecting the potential life of the foetus. Why the state may not intervene earlier is not at all clear. Is there not a potentiality of life from the very beginning of a pregnancy? It is at this point that "modern authority" enters in, modern authority in the guise of modern technology. At seven months, the foetus becomes not a person but a creature capable of surviving outside the womb. Why this creature should be capable of generating a compelling state interest that, in turn, may supersede the woman's constitutional right is, again, not made clear.

The decision was, of course, a triumph for radical feminism and its supporters. The Constitution was made to accord with their "felt desires," but we all know that these desires are not shared by everyone; and we all know that we have not seen an end to the controversy provoked.

The Constitution was also kept up to date with modern technology. But, as my friend Clifford Orwin has pointed out, technology is constantly on the march, and the Constitution may soon have to be changed radically to keep in step. Consider: the Court held that states may have a compelling state interest to protect the life of a "viable" foetus; a foetus now becomes viable—that is, capable of living outside the womb—at approximately seven months. But, as Orwin points out, on the day that the test-tube technology that produced England's Brown baby becomes general, "all abortions in the U.S. will once again fall within the purview of 'compelling state interest.' Such are the bizarre consequences of hitching your judicial wagon to a technological star."[14]

Such a decision, or such an opinion, or, if you will, such public speaking, is not calculated to persuade anyone. The opponents of abortion, the persons most in need of persuasion, have not been persuaded that their interest is illegitimate; they were told that, like the Texans in my example who want to prey upon Cuban commerce, it is an unconstitutional interest, but they do not believe it. And who can blame them for not believing it? In fact, it is in the public interest that they not believe it, for, if they were persuaded that it was the Constitution that made their interest illegitimate, they would lose whatever affection they retained for that charter of our liberties, as we used to say, and, as Madison says in *Federalist* 49, the people should revere the Constitution.

Can it be said that the friends of abortion were taught by the Court to revere, or to respect, the Constitution? I doubt it. With the assistance of the justices, they won a political victory, but, if they ponder the ruling—which, as I pointed out, rests on technology—they might see that they have reason to be apprehensive.

And for the rest of us, what were we taught by *Roe* v. *Wade*? That the Constitution is on the side of the big battalions, or, at least, the most strident battalions. That an up-to-date judiciary is contemptible because it is nothing but a political body but, unlike a political body—say, the Congress or a state legislature—it pretends not to be. And we were also taught the necessity to form battalions of our own, which, as we all know, is being done on a massive scale. The justices do not listen to constitutional argument (nor do they make it); they respond to something resembling force. They must be lobbied as legislative bodies are lobbied. Which leaves us with this question: why should we who have successfully lobbied the legislature submit to a judiciary that we cannot vote out of office? The answer to that should be, because by submitting to the judiciary we are submitting to the Constitution. Unfortunately, the judiciary has not persuaded us of this. In one sense, it does not see this as its duty; it sees its duty to be a vanguard for change. The following passage from *The Brethren* concerns a leading sex discrimination case:

> Brennen circulated [an opinion] that proposed a broad constitutional ban, declaring classification by sex virtually impermissible. He knew his alternative

14. Book review, *The University of Toronto Law Journal*, Summer 1980 (?), p. 112.

would have the effect of enacting the Equal Rights Amendment, which had already passed Congress and was pending [and at this writing is still pending] before the state legislatures. But Brennan was accustomed to having the Court out in front, leading any civil rights movement. There was no reason to wait several years for the states to ratify the amendment.[15]

Some of us have long suspected that the law clerks have a powerful influence on the justices. *The Brethren* confirms this and more: some of the decisions are written by the law clerks. Worse still, all the opinions appearing under the name of one member of the Court are written by law clerks. Law clerks are young men and women, usually from the prestigious law schools. Young persons are not given to revering anything, and our Constitution is not much in fashion in the prestigious law schools. Indeed, as I said several years ago to an audience made up almost entirely of federal judges and professors of law, the Constitution is not studied in the law schools. What is studied is constitutional law. "The difference between a course on constitutional law and a course on the Constitution is the difference between a course on the Supreme Court and a course on the principles of free government—and that difference is a measure of our problem."[16]

I have argued that, contrary to first impressions, there is properly a place for rhetoric in the judiciary. It is the means by which the people, who have passionate interests, are persuaded to moderate or forgo those interests in favor of the public interest, which is embodied in the Constitution. Because the people are still attached to the Constitution, the judiciary's rhetorical task becomes greater, if not impossible, as it departs from the constitutional text. The contemporary Supreme Court departs from the text, and in the process transforms that text, in order to adhere to the modern fashions. By doing so, rather than acting as "faithful guardians" of the Constitution, they cause the people to lose their respect for it.

15. Bob Woodward and Scott Armstrong, *The Brethren: Inside the Supreme Court* (New York: Simon and Schuster, 1979), p. 254.
16. Berns, *op. cit.*, p. 17.

# 3

# THE MEDIA WORLD AND DEMOCRATIC REPRESENTATION[1]

## HARVEY C. MANSFIELD, JR.

The media are in the middle of something—that is for certain—but of what?
They appear at first to be nothing in themselves, merely a facility of communication. They facilitate communication among a people, especially among a large
people, and thus make that people more of a people, a whole that is conscious of
itself and that, being so, can move together. We call a people of this sort a
democratic people, or simply a democracy, implying that the communication
among a people which makes possible a whole people is, or substitutes for, a form
of government. As the media facilitate communication especially among a large
people, they especially facilitate modern democracy, which, as opposed to ancient
democracy, is the democracy of a large people.

The media facilitate communication not only among a large people but also
among peoples. This they do not so much bilaterally between peoples, as if in the
manner of ambassadors with the extended but still specific mission of lying for
their country. In the recent arrest of two American reporters in Moscow, nothing
was more impressive than their greater solidarity with the editors of their newspapers than with the ambassador of their country.[2] The media facilitate communication among peoples generally without limiting themselves to specific purposes or
specific audiences. They facilitate communication among a large people only

---

1. Reprinted with permission from *Government and Opposition: A Journal of Comparative Politics*,
   Volume 14, number 3, 1979.
2. *New York Times*, 19-20 July 1978.

because it is larger than a small people, not because it is in the interest of a people to be large. A large people is preferred because it is closer to humanity itself, and it is for humanity itself that the media wish to facilitate communication. Their wish is not yet accomplished fact, and perhaps never will be. But their wish has accomplished this much: it has overcome every objection to itself in principle. While there may remain local reactionaries who grumble to their friends about the invasions of the media, all those heard on the media must speak or follow the doctrine of the media and seek to further communication among all peoples. Only through the media can mankind realize itself as the world.

With this observation, the media now appear to be not *a* facility but *the* facility of communication. As *the* facility of communication they do not merely report to a particular community the doings of that community: this is 'local news' which is of continuing concern and occasional urgency but always subordinate in importance. More than merely reporting to a given community, the media create a community by catching people's attention and holding it for events that would otherwise have taken place outside their notice. Local news may suddenly be given worldwide significance, and any individual or small group dramatically unfortunate or sufficiently determined to terrorism can be advertised to humanity. It is the media that create the 'world' in which we live and are linked to the lives of others who would never have entered our community.

When the discrepancy is seen between the people of a local community and the people of a world that the media have made or would like to make for us, and when the creative or constitutive function of the media is recognized, the dependence of the media on intellectuals can be sensed. Intellectuals provide the ideal conception of the world towards which the media, as they convey to us, convey us. What is this world and how is it governed? If the media are creative and depend on intellectuals for their communications, how can that communication be as democratic as at first appears? To answer these questions it is necessary to return to the communication of the media and to expand on the world of the intellectuals.

We must ask first, what is communicated by the media? The media do not transmit the tradition, customary belief, religion or moral standards of a community: these are for the most part still spoken face to face by parents, relatives or friends. They come from an existing community and seek to maintain that community as it has been. It would be a theoretical affectation to call such customs or mores "communication," because "communication" as opposed to speech implies a transaction that may or may not take place. Aristotle said that human beings were by nature political because they have by nature the power of speech.[3] They cannot help speaking, even in Sparta, and so they must live together chiefly on the basis of their spoken notions. But humans do not

---

3. Aristotle, *Politics*, 1253a2-18.

communicate by nature: they cannot communicate without the media which Aristotle somehow failed to mention (perhaps because he thought them identical to government or regime).

# The Fetishism of 'News'

The media, then, do not transmit custom or tradition. On the contrary, they transmit "the news." It is only human, but it is especially modern, to crave what is new. In modern times, "modern" is a term of praise; and as "modern" means new, modernity has been a movement of endless self-criticism in which any modern practice or institution, established because it was more modern than the custom that preceded it, is criticized, destroyed and replaced in accordance with its own principle by something else more modern. In keeping with the dynamism of modernity, what is known already, whether for a long time or just yesterday, is vulnerable to "the news." And the news can be 'scooped' when someone gets ahead of you and leaves you with yesterday's news.

Not everything communicated on the media is news so called, of course, but entertainment and art reflect the same avid desire for the new and exhibit the same self-cancelling principle. The latest music easily combines technical virtuosity with a graceless, unsuccessful search for the newest elemental feeling, so that we are easily apprised of the difference between a lower and a deeper feeling. The entertainment does not merely entertain, despite the disclaimers of media moguls that they mean only to entertain. Entertainment informs us of the latest trends and thus tells us what we ought to find entertaining. Although the consuming public does not swallow everything new, the skill of media entertainers is exercised to discern the public's latest preoccupation so as to make a place for themselves in it or, better, slightly beyond it. Nonetheless, the popularity of old shows on television (contemptuously called "reruns") should remind us that while modernity can deal with the *passé*, it cannot always dispose of reactionaries.

Somehow we moderns believe that the new is both more reliable and more liberating than the old, and we feel obliged to keep up with the news partly because we wish to be guided by the latest events and partly to free ourselves of dependence on yesterday's happenings. Alexander Solzhenitsyn, in his Harvard Commencement Speech criticizing the media, spoke of the people's right not to know. Anyone who has listened for a while to one of the radio stations in America now broadcasting continuous news will have an inkling of what he means, but in his formulation the idea is shocking to us.

Solzhenitsyn explains that people have a right not to have their divine souls filled with vain talk.[4] Yet the news is presented as anything but vain talk; it is grave

---

4. Alexander Solzhenitsyn, "The Exhausted West", *Harvard Magazine*, vol. 80. no. 6, July-August 1978, p. 23.

and only occasionally turns to what is called, with due solemnity, "the lighter side." The news focuses on others' troubles, of which we would know nothing or something very late and inadequate but for the media. It requires us to bear the burden of others' troubles, which is often too much for us. When peoples around the world are invited to sympathize with Angela Davis and to become indignant over her case, it is easy to suspect partisan hypocrisy; and in less well known cases of misery and oppression, we sometimes shrug our shoulders.

Thus the news provides the information that "breaks down barriers" between peoples, as it is said, and that makes "a smaller world" for us. A smaller world that is more complex, it is also said. In place of variety in the different peoples living more or less ignorant of one another, the media introduce us to complexity in their interdependence. Each people lives dependent on the fortunes of others, not merely because of commercial dealings or military threats, but also by being informed of others' fortunes. And since each people is absorbed in its inter-dependence (a more democratic word than 'dependence'), it tends to dissolve into its constituent individuals. The media direct their news at individuals rather than peoples and give them information interesting to them as human beings rather than as nationals or citizens. The media communicate in such a way as to increase communicability; they create individuals with a desire for information. They would like, it seems, to create a world of universalized information in which everyone knows the same things and wants and needs to know those things. The isolated individualism which Tocqueville saw and foresaw as the social condition of modern democracy is the ideal toward which the media are conducting us.[5]

The universality of the information provided by the media is not grounded in, or made possible by, anything outside human beings. The media are not in the middle between man and God, and altogether the men and women in the media have nothing angelic about them. In contrast to priests (who are also inter-mediaries) they do not claim to speak for God. Also, as we have seen, the media do not rest on any natural faculty of speech which would make communication possible. No universal grammar is posited which might promise a common recognition of human concerns in human speech through the variety of languages. Nor do those in the media speak Esperanto or study Latin. More than this, they do not argue or even bicker. They step across differences of language with technical terms or brand names known as Americanisms in honor of the country of origin. They do not speak to the speech of others but rather to their feelings.

If we ask what would make possible the universal communication of the media, the answer can be found in the insecurity of the human condition, our common mortality. Whatever we find surprising or disturbing is interesting news

5. Tocqueville, *Democracy in America*, D. Lawrence trans., Doubleday & Co. New York, 1969, II, II, 2-3, pp. 506-509.

to us,[6] as opposed to higher concerns of the heart and intellect which can always be postponed. But this insecurity is subject to twofold interpretation. The soft appeal of liberalism is to compassion for the suffering of others in poverty, misery or disaster; and the commentators speak easily of 'tragedy' because it is tragedy without grandeur. The harsh call of Communism is for indignation on behalf of others suffering under the oppression of poverty; here anger becomes routine. Liberalism in its present phase of soft compassion does not worry much over oppression unless it is associated with poverty, and Communism is not much concerned with poverty unless it can claim that it is caused by oppression. But both assume that neither God nor Nature demands patience or moderation in men, a recognition of their own limits, and a resignation to their ordained duties. Both assume that men can overcome their differences and be united by releasing themselves to moral feeling and giving it full scope. Only the hard-hearted (the liberals say) or only the soft-hearted (as the Communists say) stand in the way of the unification of mankind. In consequence, media commentators have the choice of shedding crocodile tears or grinding polished teeth in consonance with the appropriate universal feeling. In either case, the usual tendency is towards the Left.[7]

In Western countries, sports news provides the best reminder that mankind is divided and that pity is not the only worthy passion. Even though the results of sporting contests neither help nor hurt one's material interests (when nothing is bet), sports news is followed avidly by fans everywhere as a sign of local or national superiority. A fan of any sport shows concern for that sport wherever it is played and by whomever. But he is so distinguished from a humanitarian that to him a humanitarian appears, as it were, to be a fan of mankind in general without ever cheering for any particular team or applauding any special feat. It is in the nature of a fan both to cheer for his own side regardless of the quality of play and to applaud good or beautiful play on the other side, for modern men best appreciate in sport what the Greeks knew as noble or beautiful deeds. The media, however, do not permit their sports news to influence their view of politics. They do ensure that athletes are overpaid.

Men can communicate because they ought to communicate; but in the media formulation of the categorical imperative, no moral action is required of us as rational beings. What is communicated through the media, then, is a "news" (something new) interesting to a universal moral feeling, compassion or indignation, which divides men into individuals and then unites them without regard

6. I am indebted to Bernard Cazes for this observation.
7. Edith Efron, *The News Twisters*, Nash Publishing, Los Angeles, 1972; Leon V. Sigal, *Reporters and Officials*, D. C. Heath, Lexington, Mass., 1973; Irving Kristol, "Crisis for Journalism: The Missing Elite," in George F. Will, ed., *Press, Politics and Popular Government*, American Enterprise Institute, Washington, DC. 1972; and a forthcoming article by Stanley Rothman, "The Mass Media in Post Industrial America."

for group or national differences and without reference to any guide or standard outside men.

# Truth

Although the communication of the media is addressed to feeling, we are nonetheless compelled to ask what is the truth of what is communicated. For communication is speech after all, and if nothing true has been spoken, words have been exchanged but nothing has been communicated. The need to ask this question is confirmed by the fact that the rights and privileges of the media rest on 'the people's right to know', not on the people's need to feel. The people must be supplied with the *knowledge* they thirst for. But this must not be done in such a way as will interfere with their *judgment*, since the people have, in addition to the right to know, the right to judge. In order to respect both rights, or for some other reason, the media often convey information without accepting responsibility for its truth. They report what is said and pass on every allegation; and given the necessity of editorial selection, they can even be said to amplify human claims and assertions. The media do not respect the dignity of quiet suffering or of tolerant forbearance from claiming one's due; they favor accusers, complainers and whiners. In "editorials" they advise the people on what is true and how they should judge, but they are careful not to usurp the people's rights. When journalists claim the right to protect their sources, they say in effect that the people's right to know does not extend to a right to know the sources. But withholding the sources is justified as necessary in supplying the people with information, even though it may make such information more difficult to judge.

So the information conveyed by the media is, if not truth, a claim to truth—or perhaps better to say, a claim to be fact. The media do not state principles or develop arguments. Despite the fact that most of the news reports what is said, the media have a preference for deeds or "events" over speech. Speeches are reported as events, with neglect for the argument and with exclusive attention on the target, the upshot and the consequences. The media look for the "effectual truth" of a speech in the manner of Machiavelli, though not as acutely. For, unlike Machiavelli, they are uncritical of compassion and justice and they assume that men are free to be as soft as they please and as hard as they will. "What will happen now?" is the question to be answered. The media seek to present facts, and a fact is an event impending on the future. Whether or not facts in themselves exist, the media are concerned only with relevant facts, those relevant to our universal human feelings. The best, most factual facts are those that leave us breathless.

Facts of universal interest relevant to human suffering in poverty bespeak a philosophy of materialism. The suffering we hear of on the media is not that of the highest souls nor of the highest in ordinary men; it is the suffering —sometimes loosely called deprivation—of the poor who are poor in the goods of this world and of the body. At the same time, since the suffering is complained of, and its cause found in exploitation, there is nothing of resignation to brute matter in this materialism. The media are inspired, one might say, by an idealism of materialism, by a restless, dissatisfied materialism in which even, or especially, the rich are not happy until everyone is rich—because only the rich are happy. Idealistic materialism depends on an expanding technology to fight the war on poverty and, as regards the media, to make us aware of others' poverty so that we can become unhappy about it and deplore it.

It is obvious that the media could not exist without modern technology. Modern technology makes possible instant communication that is not face to face. Thus it leaps across the natural boundaries of rhetoric in what can be shouted to a certain, definite crowd by an orator who knows his audience. With television, modern technology even makes possible faceless communication with faces, the faces of media people who presume they know their audience from surveys and ratings. On television there is no recognition of individuality, hence no mutual recognition; there is only feedback of information. When materialism is joined to the idea of improvement, the individual matter of anyone's body matters little and enjoyment is postponed to the day when all can share in it. The only innocent enjoyment is universal, and while everyone on television is obliged to smile, it is something of a sin to laugh. One cannot laugh at the human condition—although, properly appreciated this prohibition would not permit any laughter at all. Laughter implies an undercurrent of scepticism about any social system and especially about a technological society that claims to be able to communicate despite all difficulties. Such a society pretends to be not merely not laughable, but beyond the reach of ridicule.

# Who Controls Whom?

A third question concerning the media is, who rules? Does government control the media and use it both subtly and blatantly to secure its tyrannical ends? In this case we should worry about governmental interference and try to secure the freedom and independence of the press. Or, to the contrary, is the press too powerful? According to Solzhenitsyn in the same speech at Harvard quoted before, "the press has become the greatest power within the Western countries, more powerful than the legislature, the executive, and the judiciary".[8] From this diagnosis it would follow that the media are too free, or misuse their freedom.

Clearly in the West, the media reinforce the fundamental principle of

8. Solzhenitsyn. *op. cit,*, p. 23.

modern democracy, which Tocqueville long ago discerned. This is the principle that each is capable of deciding on his own.[9] According to the media, the people have the rights to know and to judge, but these rights belong not to any definite people deciding together. They are not the rights of a people constituting itself and, as in the American Declaration of Independence, declaring itself independent so as to form a government to secure these rights. With the principle and practice of the media, it is rather that a people, indefinitely large, decides each on his own and without reference to any government, informal or formal. The government, if such there be, is merely what results from the addition of all the individual decisions, as happens in an opinion survey or an audience rating. These are decisions rather than deliberations, for as one could learn from Aristotle (or by experience), deliberation normally requires, and is improved by, the advice of other human beings.

That there need be *no common deliberation* is the most salient political consequence of the media. The media do not encourage deliberation in common; they actually discourage it by passing over every definite political or national boundary that would constitute a people in order to deliberate in common; and they themselves substitute for common deliberation in the "news" they provide to each individual regarding events outside him.[10] Common deliberation is no guarantee of a prudent result; that will depend on the prudence of those who deliberate, including their persuasiveness. But in discussion or debate, a person has to advance his cause with reasons and at least wait patiently, if not listen, while others of contrary views advance their reasons. Prejudice must be made vocal in a situation where it must meet the competition of other voices, and is thus forced to give reasons that may moderate it or take away some of its sting. If prejudice nonetheless triumphs, as it often will, at least there remains the memory of those who opposed, who "told you so," whose remarks might later stir the beginning of repentance. With information supplied by the media, however, individuals do not have to state their opinions, much less defend them. And when something goes wrong, it is easy to change one's opinion as seems necessary and convenient, without any need to explain one's principle, defend one's consistency, or swallow one's words. In deliberation, persuasion is often effected more by the character of the persuader than by the logic of his syllogisms. But known and tested character is a reasonable substitute for reason: "image," or the projecting of a perception in advance of common experience or without regard for it, is not.

What effects does the lack of common deliberation have on the practices of modern democracy? It should be admitted immediately that this lack cannot be blamed solely on the media, for the media merely actualize a principle and cul-

9. Tocqueville, *op cit.*, I, I, 5, p. 66 and I, II, 10, p. 397.
10. Paul H. Weaver, in George F. Will (ed.), *Press, Politics and Popular Government*, p. 38; and George Anastaplo, "Self-Government and the Mass Media: A Practical Man's Guide," *ibid.*, pp. 193, 197, 217.

minate a trend which, as we have noted, were observed by Tocqueville. Many other influences are at work, and perhaps ultimately one must trace the principle of each deciding on his own, as does Tocqueville, to modern philosophy.[11] Yet the media have made two effects of this principle especially evident.

First, the principle of each deciding on his own paradoxically strengthens national governments. In America it strengthens the national government as compared with local and state governments, and elsewhere in free countries, not to mention Communist countries, already powerful centralizing tendencies have been intensified. The principle that each is capable of deciding on his own, as Tocqueville again saw, does not guarantee its own success.[12] In fact, each individual is weakened by lack of support from his fellows in the family and in local or occupational associations, or in general in what have been called "mediating structures." Each unsupported individual is therefore sucked into dependence on the one source of authority that remains, the national government and national institutions. In America, radio and television are locally owned and operated, but local stations serve as outlets for syndicated programs shown everywhere, and especially for the national institutions beautifully called "networks." The press, less locally owned, operates with comparable national institutions such as the wire services and the press corps in Washington ever ready to think alike if not to deliberate together. Elsewhere in free countries, the media are even more centralized.

Even though, as has been argued above, the media are universal in character, trans-national and hence hostile to national authority, they must emanate from somewhere. Wherever the point of emanation—and it will not be a cottage in the country—it will tend to draw the attention of the audience and to have a strong, disproportionate effect on the character of the emanations. Moreover, since local influences tend to be effaced, resistance to the central sources tends to be diminished. Individuals hear little or nothing from respectable sources outside the media, at home, at work or in politics, to contradict what they receive from the media. Only their own observations, sometimes exchanged with reactionary neighbours, provide them with a just sense of stubborn self direction. But these are not given currency on the media or they are dismissed and denounced as prejudice. An individual may continue to run his own life on the basis of his own observations, but the limits within which he chooses and the general notions by which he interprets his observations are set by the media. For the most part, the sovereign individual, while never yielding his sovereignty in principle, gives himself up to the voice of the media, and the universality of the media in effect means New York, Washington and Hollywood.

Thus, to address our question about government control of the media, it is

---

11. Tocqueville, *Democracy in America*, II, I, I, pp. 429-433.
12. *Ibid,*, I, II, 5, pp. 198, 229; II, I, 2, pp. 434-435.

not so much that free governments claim sway over the media as that the media invite government control by drawing attention to themselves and by undermining institutions that might resist central authority through autonomous local control. Seeking independence from the tyranny of benighted local reactionaries, the media demand a national policy and thereby open the door to national control. National authority used as the means of liberation may be turned to the uses of indoctrination and suppression.

## How 'Open' Can a Government Be?

Yet one should not conclude from the susceptibility of the media to government control that government will be strengthened by controlling the media. While it is true that government, that is, the central or national government, may collect the actual loyalties left or created by the universalistic pretensions of the media, lending apparent strength to isolated, weakened individuals, the government may come to believe those pretensions and thus fall victim itself to the media. This is the truth in Solzhenitsyn's justifiable exaggeration regarding the power of the media as a whole. Free governments have increasingly adopted the political principle of the media, each deciding for himself on the basis of information made available by the government through the media. In America this is known as "open government."

Open government not only makes its policies clear for all to see—for all governments do this sooner or later—but also makes its policy-making clear for all to see. It is like a modern house with glass walls inside and out, including the bedroom and the bathroom. No doubt the conception of open government can be traced to Kant, not a prying man but one who believed that secrecy in government could safely and usefully be abolished. Since evil requires fraud, it begins in secrecy; and Kant wished to deny to evil the dark corners in which its plots are hatched. Today we might regard Kant's confidence in knowing evil and good as naive, but to make up for this, we assume with greater complacency than he that ignorance of evil and good does not matter. It is seemingly sufficient for the people to possess their right to know, even if in fact they cannot enjoy it because they do not or cannot know the crucial things.

In any case, open government goes beyond respecting freedom of the press to making available everything the press would like to find out, thus adopting its principle. No doubt a healthy tension remains in practice between government and the media because no government can satisfy the demand of the media for the secret behind the secret. If news is to be new, it must be a surprise; and if it is news of a policy, the surprise must be the revelation of a secret. Both government and the media have an interest in secrecy, therefore, and the tension between them is shown in a struggle as to who shall reveal the secret first. The struggle over secrecy is a struggle for sovereignty, since the sovereign power in a state is the one that has the right to act in public, shamelessly, on the basis of plans made in private. It is a sign of the media's subservience in the Soviet Union that 'news' is often announced days late, at the convenience of the government. When the media claim the right to conceal their sources from government, they claim in effect the privilege of sovereignty, or at the least, the privilege of thwarting sovereignty. Would the media have the right to penetrate the secrecy of the voting booth, where the electorate in a representative democracy exercises its sovereignty? If not, then why do they have the right to expose the secrets of the government elected by the sovereign electorate?

Solzhenitsyn and others have asked by whom the press has been elected, and to whom it is responsible?[13] Clearly the men of the media have not been elected and yet they surely claim to represent the people as much as, or more than, their elected representatives. Since the people are sovereign, they have the right to judge their elected representatives. But first they must know what their elected representatives have done or failed to do. To discover this, they must make the media their nonelective representatives armed with the people's right to know. In principle, at least, the right to know is a *carte blanche* extending into the same illegalities into which the duty to protect 'national security' is sometimes supposed to lead the executive. Thus the media's claim to check all elected government carries them above the pretension of the 'Fourth Estate' or even the 'Fourth Branch'.[14] Non-elective representation seems to be necessary for elective representation, contrary to the original hopes placed in democratic representation. There is a notion of non-elective representation abroad today which differs significantly from the notion of elective representation established in free countries during the eighteenth century.

In ancient democracies the people met together in assemblies to deliberate and decide. But they gave demagogues in those assemblies such sway over their affairs that modern theorists of popular government rejected the example and excluded assemblies of the people from the constitutions of popular governments they proposed. Instead, they adopted the principle of modern democracy, opposed to deliberation in common, that each should decide for himself. But with a view to the advantages of deliberation, they attempted to moderate that principle by instituting representative assemblies where representatives could deliberate away from the people so as not to give opportunity to demagogues. Such assemblies have had a hard job to maintain their independence. Originally their independence was established through forms of election in which the people, while

13. Solzhenitsyn, *op. cit.*, p. 23; Walter Berns, "The Constitution and a Responsible Press," in Harry M. Clor, *The Mass Media and Modern Democracy*, Rand McNally, Chicago, 1974, p. 130.
14. Douglass Cater, *The Fourth Branch of Government*, Houghton Mifflin, Boston, 1959; Marshall McLuhan, *Understanding Media*, McGraw-Hill, New York, 1964, p. 213.

exercising a choice, actually removed themselves from further choice. They chose representatives, whether legislative or executive, to choose for them. Certain forms of indirect choice were devised in which the people chose one representative which chose another, as with executive appointment of the judiciary.

# The Culmination of the Trend Towards Non-Representative Government

In time, however—in America, soon after the Constitution was established —democratic forces eroded the forms of representation which had been constructed to protect deliberation. Extra-constitutional institutions, especially parties, gained power and became dominant, in some countries using the irresistible mass power of the democratic principle against its own formal modifications. But party leaders were elected by the party membership or some portion of it, perhaps quite small. They were not elected by the people, but still they claimed to represent the people, and to represent them more faithfully and effectually than their formal, constitutional representatives. The latter had office with its formal powers, but since nothing could be done in a democracy without the people's consent, or rather, their active cooperation (for in a large country general consent lacks intensity and must be sharpened with the appetite of the interests involved), those who could rally the people—party leaders, leaders of organized interests and of social movements, journalists, *et al.*—could claim to represent them. In Communist countries the doctrine of the Party vanguard, which put the Party representing the people some distance ahead of the people, has flourished.

The media confirm and culminate the trend toward non-elective representation in democracies. More than merely checking the elected government, they attempt to by-pass representative institutions by providing "news" directly to the people to which the people are expected to give an immediate reaction. No time is given for the people's representatives to deliberate on the news, indeed their immediate reactions may also be part of the news. The news may come with an analysis provided by the media, an "instant analysis" of course, given on television particularly by persons of slick appearance and superficial education. The analysis is directed toward the question, "what will happen?"—not to the question of deliberation, "what shall we do?" The reaction of the people reported as part of the news, is similarly undeliberative; the question put to them, in contempt for their right to know, is not "what do you think?" but "how do you feel?" Answers to this question may vary, but the people come to consensus, without deliberating, by means of surveys. Here their responses are added up and put in order not by elected representatives but by clerks, statisticians, public opinion experts and other weighty but undeliberative analysts.

In by-passing formal representative institutions, the media also tend to replace earlier, informal institutions, such as parties and organized interest groups, that also by-passed those institutions. It may be correct to say that the newest of the media, television, has by-passed the oldest, the press. While the rights of a free press were first established to promote the deliberation of a free people, they have now been extended to television and increasingly used in practices hostile to deliberation.[15] At the same time newspapers more and more seek to resemble television and to overcome, with "advocacy journalism," "journalese" and populistic moralism, the formal barriers to democratization imposed by the written word.

Much of the self-justification of the media—that they make democracy more open and more democratic—remind an observer of the self-justification of parties and the press at their inception; and much of the criticism of the media reminds one likewise of early attacks upon parties and the press. The media accuse the other non-elective representative institutions of being unresponsive to the people, and in their way they are right. As democracy becomes more democratic, it becomes more informal. Forms of election, in particular, disappear; for election, as Aristotle noted, is an aristocratic principle.[16] It is also true that one does not get rid of leaders and "elites" simply by attacking, undermining or ignoring the leaders who have been elected. Informal leaders spring up like weeds to replace the deposed formal leaders, and doubt remains whether democracy can survive if it rushes towards more democracy by neglect of the forms of democracy.

To whom, then, are the informal leaders of the media responsible? They are responsive (informally) but not responsible (formally) to the people. They are not, perhaps, responsible to intellectuals, but they are dependent on them. Precisely because those in the media are persons of slight education, they depend on the intellectuals whom they surpass in beauty and income. They sense that "news" looks to the future but they cannot see with their tongues, as can intellectuals. The meaning of the news escapes them. Since the news communicates everything, and makes everything communicable, the latest trends in thought, in economics and even in cosmology, which once were held of interest only to philosophers, must be communicated to the people; and only intellectuals can do this without being subjected to derision. Intellectuals must tell us what is behind the latest anti-inflation policy or the space program. Theory has become confused with practice in the realm of technology, where theory has practical results and practice changes with new theoretical discoveries. The media men, who live on nothing if not technology, are hardly in a position to boast of their common sense to distinguish themselves from intellectuals. They are city slickers *par excellence*. If they communicate anything, they must communicate information

15. Anastaplo, *op. cit.*, p. 195; McLuhan, *op. cit.*, chs. 21. 31.
16. Aristotle, *Politics*, 1273a27, 1294b9.

to the uninformed, that is, sophistication to the unsophisticated. They therefore depend on the sources of sophistication.

Perhaps the best example of this dependence is the media's promotion, apparently against their own interest, of the intellectuals' disdain for technology. The media stop short of endorsing the intellectuals' attacks on themselves. But they go out of their way to report criticism of modern industry, products and corporations—though not criticism of modern art, music and books. They share, without understanding, the intellectuals' (not unreasonable) doubt that rational control of the world through technology is possible, or if possible, productive of good for mankind. Dating from Rousseau, this doubt has in time acquired much of the sophistication it was originally directed against, and the doubters now express themselves over the media with media amplification of uncertain but sincere fidelity.

Meanwhile, the intellectuals from their side depend on the media. The world of media communication we have described is in fact the world of the intellectuals. Their world excludes the fundamental principle of the ancient philosophers that thinking requires, and makes possible, detachment from one's "worldly" concerns. The world of the intellectuals is *this* world, the world of worldly concern; and therefore it contains a place, not too modest, for the intellectuals themselves. They are not above it all; they are no strangers to wealth and fame; they do not lack the desire to rule.

Whether in fact intellectuals rule the world they interpret may well be doubted. Politics has its own imperatives that do not respond to direction from above. Moreover, the world of the intellectuals appears to be divided in contradiction, as we have seen, between the news we are filled with and its meaning, which we are ignorant of, between the right to know and the lack of knowledge. How can intellectuals maintain their status if they admit that information has replaced deliberation and no longer assert that the intellect elevates them above others? To reflect on this question, a philosopher is needed.

# 4

# THE RHETORIC OF ALEXANDER HAMILTON

## FORREST MCDONALD

The political rhetoric of the Founders of the American Republic has received scant attention from scholars. The relative neglect is understandable. On the one hand, the very concept of rhetoric has, in modern times, all but lost its classical signification, and has come to mean empty verbosity or ornament. On the other, the political achievements of the Founders—the winning of independence, the establishment of a durable federal Union on republican principles, the creation of a system of government which is itself bound by law—were of such monumental proportions as to make their methods of persuasion seem of pedantic and picayune consequence. And thus, though every student of the epoch is at least vaguely aware that the general level of public discourse in late eighteenth-century America was extraordinarily high, perhaps unprecedentedly so, we tend to regard the way the Founders spoke and wrote as only incidental to what they did. I would contend, on the contrary, that it was their commitment to and practice of open, dispassionate, informed, and reasoned discussion of public questions which made their achievements possible. Their rhetoric, in other words, was not a mere by-product of their accomplishments: rather, their accomplishments were the product of their rhetorical interchange.

In the most general proper sense of the term, rhetoric is the art of persuasion through written or spoken language. In the classical and eighteenth-century usage, however, it meant persuasion according to certain formal rules. The Founding Fathers studied and practiced the art in accordance with the Aristotelian model, and at the risk of boring those of you who know far more about the subject than I do, I shall begin by pointing out a couple of the implications inherent in that model.[1]

First, Aristotle ruled out the relationship of rhetoric to pure knowledge, insisting instead that, since it was founded upon opinion rather than upon absolute truth, it was concerned only with matters of probability. I shall clarify that point later. For now, what is important is that consciousness of that limitation of the art was of immense value in the building of American republican institutions, for it meant that public discourse could not be conducted in terms of ideological certainties of the sort that perverted the French Revolution and, indeed, most other revolutions. Instead, discussion of public questions was at its best a trial-and-error process of moving toward ever-greater probabilities of truth without succumbing to the fatal sin of gnosticism, the belief that one has arrived at absolute Truth.

Second, though the rules required that persuasion be based on reasoned argument, they permitted two additional forms of "proof" besides logical proof. These were ethical proof, which was designed to win from the audience a favorable attitude toward the author or speaker, and emotional proof, which was aimed at putting the audience in a receptive frame of mind. Given the Founding Fathers' understanding that men are governed by their passions—that is, drives for self-gratification—and by habits and sentiments, and that reason is normally the servant rather than the master of the passions, this meant that their rhetoric and their view of the nature of man could complement and reinforce one another. It also meant that they were enabled to (as they were obliged to) work toward raising the level of public sentiments as well as the level of public understanding. This was put simply and clearly by the celebrated author of the 1767 *Letters from a Farmer in Pennsylvania*, John Dickinson. In his seventh letter Dickinson quotes at length from speeches that Lord Camden and William Pitt had given in Parliament, praises the "generous zeal for the rights of mankind that glows in every sentence," and analyzes what it was that made their rhetoric so powerful: "Their reasoning is not only just—it is, as Mr. *Hume* says of the

1. In my comments on Aristotelian rhetoric, I have been guided by Larry Arnhart's paper, "The Federalist as Aristotelian Rhetoric," presented at the Annual Meeting of the Midwest Political Science Association (Chicago, 1979). Professor Arnhart kindly supplied me with a copy. I find his argument that the Founding Fathers followed the Aristotelian model entirely convincing. His forthcoming "Aristotle on Political Reasoning: A Commentary on the *Rhetoric*" is scheduled for publication by Northern Illinois University Press in 1981. See also Bower Aly, *The Rhetoric of Alexander Hamilton* (New York, 1941).

eloquence of Demosthenes, 'vehement.' It is disdain, anger, boldness, freedom, involved in a continual stream of argument."[2]

Historians, in dealing with the Founding Fathers, have paid too much attention to the "justice of their reasoning" and not enough to their "vehemence." If a proper balance were brought to a study of the writings of the founders, I believe, the result would be an enormous contribution to our understanding of them. If I were outlining such a study, I would suggest a rhetorical analysis of a half-dozen patriotic tracts written between the 1760s and 1776: Dickinson's *Letters*, John Adams's *Novanglus Letters*, James Wilson's *Considerations on the ... Authority of the British Parliament*, Thomas Jefferson's *Summary View of the Rights of British America*, Thomas Paine's *Common Sense*, and the Declaration of Independence.

I would also suggest that the student be sensitive to certain nuances of eighteenth-century political writing which have eluded most investigators. One concerns the meaning of words. The meaning of many crucial words has changed so radically that, without an *Oxford English Dictionary* at one's side, one is likely to commit grave errors of interpretation. In a moment I shall offer some fairly dramatic examples of the ways that meanings have changed; meanwhile, a related subtlety is that there were then, as there are now, a variety of code words in common currency. For instance, there was the phrase "Great Man." In one of my early books I missed entirely the connotations of the phrase: having noticed that it was frequently used to describe the financier of the Revolution, Robert Morris, I misread it to mean that even Morris's enemies viewed him with a touch of awe. Much later I learned that it had been used by English Oppositionists as a contemptuous description of Sir Robert Walpole, then applied to the corrupt and wealthy aristocrats who dominated English politics in mid-century. It was the Oppositionists' ideological heirs in America, anti-Federalists and Jeffersonian Republicans, who applied the term to Morris—as they did also to Hamilton and Washington—and they were using it as a form of condemnation.[3] Finally, there are literary conventions which can sometimes be revealing. For example, pre-Revolutionary political tracts abounded in typographical variations—the use of italics, all capital letters, and extravagant

2. Forrest McDonald, ed., *Empire and Nation: Letters from a Farmer in Pennsylvania, John Dickinson, Letters from the Federal Farmer, Richard Henry Lee* (Englewood Cliffs, N.J., 1962), 45n.
3. Forest McDonald, *We the People: The Economic Origins of the Constitution* (Chicago. 1958), 54; Rodger D. Parker, *The Gospel Of Opposition: A Study in Eighteenth Century Anglo-American Ideology* (Ph.D.. dissertation, Wayne State University, 1975); Harvey Mansfield, Jr., *Statesmanship and Party Government: A study of Boire and Bolingiere* (Chicago 1765); Philadelphia *Freeman's Journal*, October 10, 1783; George Clinton to John Lamb, June 28, 1788, quoted in Aly, *Rhetoric of Hamilton.* 164n; Edgar S. Maclay, ed., *Journal of William Maclay United States Senator from Pennsylvania, 1789-1791* (New York, 1890).

punctuation—designed to achieve emphasis, indicating that the authors were thinking in terms of speech to small, tangible audiences. Upon the emergence of a truly national politics and the large, impersonal audience that that implied, typographical variations were abandoned, indicating that the writers now intended their words to be read rather than heard.[4]

Enough of preaching: it is time to start practicing. I have been speaking of a study that someone should make; let us turn to one that I have made, of the rhetoric of Alexander Hamilton. As we do so, we immediately face three formidable obstacles, all of which arise from Hamilton's historical reputation. It is commonly alleged that Hamilton was contemptuous of public opinion; that he created a system based upon greed, in disdain of public spiritedness; and that he was hypocritical, saying one thing in private and another in public. These allegations, if true, would make analysis of his rhetoric pointless, save perhaps as an exercise in the study of duplicity. Each must therefore be considered before we proceed.

The first allegation rests mainly on a misreading of Hamilton's language. After the Whiskey Rebellion in 1794, Hamilton said in a letter to Washington that he had "long since ... learnt to hold popular opinion of no value." If those words are read in their twentieth-century sense, they are pretty damning, and they seem conclusive; and that is the sense in which historians have read them. Richard K. Kohn, for instance, though usually a careful scholar, quotes Hamilton's remark, adds that President Washington "knew he could not govern on such principles," and cites with approval Secretary of State Edmund Randolph as saying that "Hamilton's ideas 'would heap curses upon the government. The strength of a government is the affection of the people.'"[5]

But let us consider Hamilton's language more carefully. The operative words are "popular" and "opinion." I do not have space here (even if I knew enough) to do full justice to the etymology of the word "popular" or to the historical distinction between it and the word "public," but I can summarize briefly. In its ancient forms and in its seventeenth and eighteenth century usage, "popular" comprehended everybody; in meaning, though not in its roots, it was akin to "common" or "vulgar." It also had a specific political connotation, namely left-wing (significantly, Hamilton's remark was apropos political attacks

---

4. The change is readily observed by comparing Dickinson's essays with Lee's in McDonald, ed., *Empire and Nation.*
5. Hamilton to Washington, November 11, 1794, in Harold C. Syrett, ed., *The Papers of Alexander Hamilton* (26 vols., New York, 1961-1979), 17:366; Richard H. Kohn, *Eagle and Sword: The Federalists and the Creation of the Military Establishment in America, 1783-1802* (New York, 1975), 172.

in Philip Freneau's left-wing newspaper, *The National Gazette*). "Public," by contrast, was derived from the same root as the word pubic, meaning manhood; it referred individually to those who had attained the full status and responsibilities of manhood and referred collectively to the political society or body politic itself. Interestingly, "virtue"—which Montesquieu and others regarded as the actuating principle of a *republic*—was also derived from a root word meaning manhood. Thus the phrases "public virtue" and "republican virtue," which had considerable currency in eighteenth century America, were somewhat tautological, whereas "popular virtue" would have been a contradiction in terms, the component words being mutually exclusive. As for the word "opinion," it was used in at least three distinct ways in the eighteenth century. One was the Aristotelian usage, as a technical term associated with probability, with the assembly and the courts, and thus with rhetoric. More frequently, it was used in the present sense, meaning belief or prejudice. Still a third usage signified confidence, esteem, and high regard. Following an essay by David Hume, Hamilton had indicated in the Constitutional Convention that he used the term in the third sense. In other words, he was saying in 1794 that he held it of no value to be well-regarded by the rabble and by rabble-rousers—or, to phrase it differently, that statesmanship is not a popularity contest.[6]

That is a far cry from expressing contempt for what the public thinks and believes. Hamilton made his meaning clearer in the rest of his letter to Washington: after saying that he had learned to hold popularity of no value, he added that his reward for service to the public would be in "the esteem of the discerning and in internal consciousness of zealous endeavours for the public good." Historians have somehow managed to omit that part of his letter, just as they have managed to ignore the fact that Hamilton probably expended more energy, thought, and words trying to create and guide an informed public opinion than did any of his contemporaries.

The second allegation, that Hamilton's policies represented an effort to build a political system on greed rather than on civic virtue, stemmed from more complex roots. It originated in the charges of his political enemies. Some (William Maclay, for example) were economically interested in discrediting Hamilton; others (Jefferson and Madison, for example) were politically interested in doing so; still others (John Taylor of Caroline, for example) were ideologically interested in doing so. But that view of Hamilton has also been expounded by an impressive array of modern scholars including E. James Ferguson, Gerald Stourzh, J.G.A. Pocock, and, most recently, Drew R. McCoy. The eighteenth century, as these historians have pointed out, witnessed the

6. This analysis is based upon *The Oxford English Dictionary*, supplemented by many years of study of usages in eighteenth-century political writings. I have been given informative suggestions on earlier usages by my colleague, Professor Michael Mendle.

development of a school of political theory that espoused what Pocock calls "the movement from virtue to interest" as the activating principle of government: it began with Bernard de Mandeville's *Fable of the Bees* (1714), holding that private vice was the wellspring of public virtue, and ran through Adam Smith and his often-quoted passage which begins, "It is not from the benevolence of the butcher, the brewer or the baker that we expect our dinner, but from their regard of their own interest." According to McCoy, the "powerful, economically advanced modern state" which Hamilton envisaged "would stand squarely on the worldly foundations of 'corruption' that Bernard Mandeville had spoken of." [7]

The case is persuasive. Though Hamilton never read Mandeville, as far as I am aware, he did read and on several occasions quote from David Hume's essays in a similar vein, and he read and was influenced by Adam Smith. Moreover, in 1783 he clearly advocated the consolidation of national authority through appeals to the interests of public creditors and financial and commercial groups, and in 1784 he said flatly that "the safest reliance of every government is on men's interest." I myself have been guilty of writing that Hamilton's program as Secretary of the Treasury depended upon tying the interests of public creditors to the fate of his measures. [8]

But I was wrong, and so are the others. Two things happened to Hamilton between 1783 and 1789 which radically altered his thinking on this subject: he learned from observing and participating in state politics that state governments could be more effective in employing avarice to win political support than could a national government, and he learned from study of the principles of natural law that morality, in the long run, was a more stable foundation for government than was economic self-interest. Despite the abundance of charges, there is no evidence whatsoever that Hamilton used the lure of personal gain in seeking congressional support for his measures. Moreover, he expressed himself clearly on the subject in a remarkable private document he wrote in 1795. In drafting his plan for assuming the state debts, he admitted, he had taken into account the tendency of assumption "to strengthen our infant Government by increasing the number of ligaments between the Government and the interests of Individuals.... Yet upon the whole it was the consideration upon which I relied least of

7. E. James Ferguson. "The Nationlist of 1781-1783 and the Economic Interpretation of the Constitution," in *Journal of American History*, 60:241-261 (1969-1970); Gerald Stoursh, *Alexander Hamilton and the Idea of Republican Government* (Stanford, 1970); J. G. A. Pocock, *The Machiavellian Moment* (Princetor, NJ. 1975), 531; Drew R. McCoy, *The Elusive Republic: Political Economy in Jeffersonian America* (Chapel Hill, 1980), 13-47, 133. The Smith quotation is in the condensed version of *The Wealth of Nations* edited by Bruce Mazlish (Indianapolis, 1961), 15; it is found in Book 1, Chapter 2.

8. First Letter from Phocion, January 1784, in Syrott, ed., *Papers of Hamilton*, 3:494; Forrest McDonald, *The Presidency of George Washington* (Lawrence, Kansas, 1974), 67.

all." Even on purely practical grounds, had this been "the weightiest motive to
the measure, it would never have received my patronage." And, he added in a
marginal note to himself, "such means are not to be resorted to but the good
sense & virtue of the people."[9]

The third common allegation against Hamilton, that he was hypocritical in
his public utterances—and most particularly, that he spoke contemptuously of
"the people" in private and sang a different tune for public consumption—is
likewise without foundation. It is true that, in his youthful disillusionment with
the way the Revolutionary War was going, he expressed his disgust with the
people. In 1779 he wrote his intimate friend Henry Laurens that "the birth and
education of these states has fitted their inhabitants for the chain, and ... the
only condition they sincerely desire is that it may be a golden one." The next
year he wrote Laurens that "Our countrymen have all the folly of the ass and
the passiveness of the sheep in their composition.... The whole is a mass of
fools and knaves." In maturity, however, he arrived at a different and more
balanced view and expressed it in public and private alike. I shall return to that
later. Meanwhile, the measure of his duplicity, or lack of it, is to be found in
comparing his public writings, from *The Federalist Papers* through the 1790s,
with his private correspondence. Such comparison reveals a record of virtually
perfect consistency. The truth is that Hamilton was, as Fisher Ames said of him,
"the most frank of men"; and, as he said of himself in a letter to an intimate
friend, "what I would not promulge I would avoid ... pride makes it part of my
plan to *appear truly what I am.*" Indeed, his passion for candor more than once
led him to transcend the boundaries of prudence—as he did, for instance, in
publishing the details of his sexual affair with Maria Reynolds so as to protect
the integrity of the office he had filled.[10]

Hamilton's rhetoric may be fruitfully examined by considering separately
his employment of each of the Aristotelian forms of proof. Thorough analyses
of two of his performances have been made along those lines: Bower Aly's study
of Hamilton's speeches in the New York ratifying convention, published in
1941, and Larry Arnhart's study of the rhetoric of *The Federalist*, delivered

9. The Defence of the Funding System (July, 1795) in Syrett, ed., *Papers of Hamilton*, 19:40-41.
   Regarding Hamilton's growth and maturity in the 1780s, see Forrest McDonald, *Alexander
   Hamilton: A Biography* (New York, 1979), 49-94.
10. Hamilton to Laurens, September 11, 1779, June 30, September 12, 1780, to Robert Troup,
   April 13, 1795, in Syrett, ed., *Papers of Hamilton*, 2:167, 347, 428. 18:329; Ames to Rufus King
   (July 15, 1800) in Charles R. King. ed., *The Life and Correspondence of Rufus King*, 3:275-276
   (New York, 1894); McDonald, Hamilton, 227-230, 237, 243-244, 259, 334-336.

before the Midwest Political Science Association in 1979. Some of what I have to say in the following pages draws on these two studies.

Logical proof, as opposed to ethical and emotional proof, carries the greatest portion of the burden in Hamilton's rhetoric. Let me pause here to say, for the benefit of those who are nonspecialists—and particularly for those who, like my wife, respond to the esoteric language of philosophical abstractions with a glazed eye and a deaf ear—that I shall try to keep this as simple as possible. Logical reasoning is of two broad kinds: deductive, which means reasoning from general propositions to arrive at particular conclusions, and inductive, which means reasoning from a number of particular observations to arrive at general propositions. The principal device of deductive reasoning is called a syllogism, and it is something we all employ even if we have never heard the word. A syllogism consists, in order, of 1) a major premise, 2) a minor premise, and 3) a conclusion, as in this example: 1) no man is immortal. 2) John Smith is a man, and 3) therefore John Smith is not immortal.

But deductive reasoning in rhetoric, though having the same structure as that in other forms of logic, is not quite the same in substance. In rhetorical reasoning, one uses a special kind of syllogism called an enthymeme. The main difference between a pure syllogism and an enthymeme is in the nature of the major premise. In a pure syllogism the major premise is absolutely true, as in "the square of the hypotenuse of a right triangle equals the sum of the squares of the other two sides." In an enthymeme, the major premise is based instead upon the reputable beliefs of the audience, which are only probably and relatively true, as in the statements "people are creatures of habit," or "honesty is the best policy."

Hamilton described the two kinds of premises, as well as deductive reasoning as he practiced it, in *Federalist 31*. "In disputations of every kind," he said at the beginning of that essay, "there are certain primary truths or first principles upon which all subsequent reasonings must depend. These contain an internal evidence, which antecedent to all reflection or combination commands the assent of the mind.... Of this nature are the maxims in geometry, that 'the whole is greater than its part,'" and so on. "Of the same nature are those other maxims in ethics and politics, that there cannot be an effect without a cause; that the means ought to be proportioned to the end; that every power ought to be commensurate with its object; that there ought to be no limitation of a power destined to effect a purpose, which is itself incapable of limitation."[11]

A couple of aspects of this description want special notice. One is that Hamilton tends, in the passage quoted, to treat the two kinds of premises as equally valid. Doing so was an effective rhetorical device as well as a reflection

11. Federalist Number 31, in Syrett, ed., *Papers of Hamilton*, 4:456. Arnhart analyzes this argument in "The Federalist as Aristotelian Rhetoric," 15-16.

of his personality—he was nothing if not positive and forceful—but he knew the difference. The first kind was what, elsewhere, he called "geometrically true," the other what he called "morally certain." The second subtle aspect of the passage quoted is that there is a progression in his examples of "maxims in ethics and politics," from one which nobody would question to one that many members of his audience might challenge. The listing itself is almost a process of deduction. That, too, was both an effective rhetorical device and a reflection of his personality.

As for Hamilton's inductive reasoning—that is, reasoning from experience, observation, or example—he always employed it, his mixture of inductive and deductive varying with the audience. Temperamentally, he distrusted the deductive and preferred the inductive, "A great source of error," he wrote early in his career, "is the judging of events by abstract calculations, which though geometrically true are false as they relate to the concerns of beings governed more by passion and prejudice than by an enlightened sense of their interests." In *Federalist 20*, echoing a sentiment shared by most of the Founding Fathers, he and Madison said that "Experience is the oracle of truth; and where its responses are unequivocal, they ought to be conclusive and sacred." In any event, as Arnhart has pointed out, he made clear to his audience whether he was using one or the other or both by introducing his arguments with such phrases as "theory and practice conspire to prove."[12]

I shall not go into a detailed analysis of all the rhetorical techniques Hamilton employed in his logical proof. Aly has done so at great length, in regard to speech after speech. Aly points out where Hamilton has employed dilemma, antecedent probability, analogy, exposure of inconsistency, reduction to absurdity, causal relation, turning the tables, and other devices. For those who are interested in pursuing the matter further. I recommend Aly's work heartily.

But there are three additional aspects of Hamilton's method of using rhetorical logic which, while compatible with the Aristotelian model, were unique to him. One was that his approach was always positive, never negative. As the editors of his law papers put it, "His habit of thought even when acting for the defense was affirmative; in other words, he was always carrying the war to the enemy." That habit reflected his personality, but it was also a deliberate choice of rhetorical strategy and tactics. In this regard, it is instructive to observe the brief notes Hamilton recorded from Demosthenes' Orations (which

12. *Ibid.*, 17-18; Hamilton to ——, December 1779, and Federalist 20, in Syrett, ed., *Papers of Hamilton*, 2:242, 4:395. Arnhart (p. 19) points out that Publius uses two kinds of experience, that derived from the study history and that derived from observation of ongoing affairs. He does not point out—what close analysis of *The Federalist* reveals—that Madison was much more given to citing historical examples, Hamilton to citing current and recent experience.

he studied while in the army). " 'Where attack him, it will be said? Ah Athenians, war, war itself will discover to you his weak sides, if you will seek them.' Sublimely simple." And again, "As a general marches at the head of his troops, so ought wise politicians, if I dare to use the expression, to march at the head of affairs; insomuch that they ought not to await the *event*, to know what measures to take; but the measures which they have taken, ought to produce the *event.*" In addition to being effective, this positive style had a special advantage that is related to the inner logic of rhetorical reasoning. The speaker or writer is limited, in attempting to persuade his audience, by the fact that the premises from which he can argue are restricted to what the audience already accepts as an established truth. Hamilton's practice of seeking the enemy's weak sides and seizing the initiative "to produce the event" enabled him to broaden the range of acceptable premises, and thus to educate as well as to persuade his audiences.[13]

The second of Hamilton's special qualities was an intuitive sense of the heart of a subject combined with an awesome capacity for mastering its details. As William Pierce wrote of him in the Constitutional Convention, "he enquires into every part of his subject with the searchings of philosophy ... there is no skimming over the surface of a subject with him, he must sink to the bottom to see what foundation it rests on ... and when he comes forward he comes highly charged with interesting matter." His speeches and writings were characteristically long, for he was rarely content to rely upon only one approach to an argument, even when he was confident of winning in a single stroke. His celebrated opinion on the constitutionality of the bank affords an excellent example. He disposes of Randolph's and Jefferson's arguments in six brief but devastating paragraphs—piercing immediately to the heart of their position, showing the false premise on which it rests, indicating the appropriate premise, and drawing from it the only reasonable conclusion. But then he goes on for another 15,000 words, ringing every imaginable change on the argument. The beauty of this technique is again its educational value: it goes beyond successful persuasion in the particular instance and establishes new foundations for further persuasion on the morrow.[14]

Hamilton's third special quality is more difficult to describe. He was sensitive to the difference between the two nontechnical connotations of the word opinion: belief, judgment, prejudice on the one hand, approval, esteem, regard

13. Julius Coebel, Jr., and others, eds., *The Law Practice of Alexander Hamilton: Documents and Commentary,* 1:3 (New York, 1964); Hamilton's Pay Book notes (1777) in Syrett, ed., *Papers of Hamilton,* 1:390.
14. Max Farrand, ed., Records of the Federal Convention of 1787 (4 vols., New Haven, 1937), 3:89; Opinion on the Constitutionality of an Act to Establish a Bank (February 23) 1791, in Syrett, ed., *Papers of Hamilton,* 8:97-134. Aly comments on Hamilton's practice of ringing the changes on the arguments in his speeches in the New York ratifying convention: *Rhetoric of Hamilton,* 171 and elsewhere.

on the other. In conventional rhetorical theory, it was opinion in the first sense, belief, that supplied the premises for deductive logical proof; opinion in the second sense, approval, would fall under ethical proof, having to do with the audience's favorable view of the author or speaker. Hamilton perceived that in the circumstances in which he labored—the attempt to establish a durable republican system of government—the two were so interrelated as to be inseparable. Each supported the other: the tasks of winning belief and approval went hand in hand. As a statesman he was seeking to establish public "credit" in the broad sense of credibility or confidence as well as in the narrow financial sense; indeed, in some respects he viewed the latter as only a means of attaining the former. Moreover—and this is crucial—he understood that opinions derive as much from perceptions as they do from facts. "A degree of illusion mixes itself in all the affairs of society," he wrote; "The opinion of objects has more influence than their real nature." Or, as he said in his First Report on the Public Credit. "In nothing are appearances of greater moment, than in whatever regards credit. Opinion is the soul of it, and this is affected by appearances, as well as realities." There is an extremely subtle point here: one central aim of Hamilton's public life was to replace the prevailing law of contract, based upon the medieval concepts of just price and fair value, with a modern theory of contract based upon consent in a free market. Thus Hamilton's attention to the effect of appearances on opinion, like his other two special qualities, was an extension of the dimensions of logical proof, for it broadened the possible range of premises available within the rules of reasoning with enthymemes.[15]

Most of the techniques I have been describing can be illustrated by a brief analysis of one of Hamilton's greatest performances, the *Report on Manufactures* presented to Congress in December, 1791. The rhetorical situation was different from what it had been when Hamilton had given his reports on the public credit and the bank. On the earlier occasions the audience agreed with the first premise, that it was imperative to establish a system of public credit; Hamilton's task of persuasion was to convince Congress that it was desirable to do so in a particular way. In regard to the *Report on Manufactures*, the body of beliefs shared by most members of the audience, which we may describe in shorthand as the agrarian ideal, was hostile to Hamilton's objective, the promotion of industry. His task of persuasion was to convince Congress that it was desirable to encourage manufacturing, whatever the means.

He began by isolating and attacking the enemy's weakest side. The agrarian ideal itself was an impregnable bastion of prejudice, but the economic theory used to justify it—the physiocrat's rather silly notion that land is the

---

15. The quotations in this paragraph are from Hamilton to ——, December, 1779, and Report Relative to a Provision for the Support of Public Credit, January 9, 1790, in Syrett, ed., *Papers of Hamilton*, 2:242, 6:97. The generalizations are my own, derived from long study of Hamilton.

source of all wealth and that the labor of craftsmen adds nothing to the value of things—was highly vulnerable. Hamilton demolished the physiocratic theory by quoting and paraphrasing at length from Adam Smith's *Wealth of Nations*, a work whose free-trade doctrines the audience regarded with great respect. He was careful, however, not to draw any conclusions beyond what his argument demonstrated: all he claimed at that stage was that manufacturing could produce wealth, probably about equally with farming.

Hamilton's rhetorical strategy so far, that of using one body of acceptable premises to displace another, was effective, but it created a new rhetorical problem. The use of Smith's work had the advantage of establishing as premises for further argument, that the wealth of a nation could be increased. On the other hand, it also had a disadvantage, for Hamilton was advocating active government promotion of manufactures, and Smith had championed the doctrine of noninterference—the idea that human industry, "if left to itself, will naturally find its way to the most useful and profitable employment." To overcome that difficulty, Hamilton again sought the weakest sides of the argument. Smith, as Hamilton paraphrased him, had laid down seven new premises to prove that manufacturing could increase the wealth of a nation—the principle of the division of labor, the advantages of the use of machinery, the possibility of enlarging the labor pool by pulling normally idle people into it, and so on. As Hamilton developed each point, he corrected Smith by using inductive rather than deductive reasoning, which is to say by employing the awesome array of factual data which Hamilton had laboriously gathered for the purpose. By that means he transformed Smith's premises into his own. To put it another way, he had taken premises acceptable to the audience, from which it was not logically possible to conclude that governmental activism was desirable, and altered them in such a way that it could logically be shown that such activism was not only desirable but in fact necessary.

Now Hamilton brought the cumulative effects of previous argumentation into play. Given the proposition that manufacturing should be encouraged, the fact remained that the United States, as an undeveloped country, was woefully short of the necessary capital. That obstacle was readily overcome, Hamilton said, and he showed how by reviewing his reports on public credit, where he had demonstrated that the public debt could be institutionally manipulated in such a way that, with the support of public opinion, it would be turned into a great pool of liquid wealth or capital. From there to the end of the report, Hamilton had smooth sailing: all he had to do was propose a series of practical steps to be taken to bring about the desired ends.

I described the *Report on Manufactures* as one of Hamilton's greatest performances. The historians among you, however, will recall that Congress did not act on the report; and the rhetoricians, armed with that datum, will conclude that the performance was not a great one at all. Let me construct the enthymeme: excellent rhetoric persuades the audience, Hamilton's report failed to persuade the audience, and therefore the report was not excellent rhetoric. But Hamilton's audience did not consist exclusively of the members of the Second Congress. In his rhetoric as in his statesmanship, Hamilton was addressing posterity and building cumulatively toward the future. In the course of time, the nation would begin the active promotion of manufactures, and for more than a century Hamilton's report would provide the rhetorical foundation for such a policy. Indeed, the report itself became a first premise.

There remains the task of reviewing briefly Hamilton's use of ethical and emotional proof and, finally, his style. In regard to the first two I shall depend, for my theoretical underpinnings, largely on Arnhart, for he has put the matter extremely well. For the last I shall return exclusively to my own analysis, for there is an important dimension to Hamilton's style which he and others have overlooked.

Since the time of John Locke, logicians and rhetoricians have tended to share Plato's suspicion of traditional rhetoric because of its admission of irrational appeals to the audience. If ethical and emotional proofs are made in adherence to Aristotle's standards, however, they can in fact contribute to rational discourse. As for ethical proof, Aristotle says that a speaker will be most persuasive if he shows himself to be possessed of prudence, virtue, and good will. The persuasiveness of a speaker's character, based upon those criteria, can scarcely be dismissed as irrational: it is obviously quite reasonable to judge the reliability of a writer or speaker as being proportionate to his prudence, his virtue, and his good will. Besides, the more an author or speaker establishes his own credentials on those foundations, the more he conditions the audience to expect and demand them of other authors and speakers—and thus contributes to raising the general level of the rationality of the audience, which in turn elevates the rational possibilities available to the author or speaker.[16]

Hamilton's use of ethical proof was calculated to obtain just that end. His techniques varied with his audience, of course, as they necessarily must. In dealing with Washington, for instance, the appropriate tone was one of deference —not of flattery, which the president would instantly have regarded as showing an absence of character, but out of respect for the presidential office and for the president's own character. In other words, one gained Washington's respect by showing respect in a proper manner. Washington was a special case, but in a sense that was the way Hamilton employed ethical proofs in more conventional rhetorical situations. That is to say, Hamilton normally sought to establish his good character among the members of his audience not by reciting his own

16. Arnhart, "The Federalist as Aristotelian Rhetoric", 22-24.

virtues but by appealing to theirs. He appealed to his audiences to judge his arguments dispassionately, openly, and in a spirit of moderation tempered by zealous concern for the happiness of their country. By urging them to be prudent, virtuous, and possessed of good will, he avoided the necessity of claiming to have those qualities himself; and to the extent that he succeeded, he actually instilled them in his audiences.[17]

As for emotional proofs, they are legitimate in Aristotle's scheme of things only insofar as the passions with which they deal are rational ones. Now, passions are passions and reason is reason, to be sure; but passions can be short-sighted or prudent, biased or open, hastily formed or carefully considered. After all, there is such a thing as reasonable fear, and in some circumstances to be unafraid is to be unreasonable. Hamilton sometimes appealed to the fears of his audience, as when, in numerous of the *Federalist* essays, he declared that failure to adopt the Constitution would result in anarchy, tyranny, and war—and when, in essays on the French Revolution, he warned of the perils of emotional or ideological attachment to foreign powers. There are those of us who believe those fears were entirely reasonable. More characteristically, however, Hamilton's appeals were to noble and positive passions: pride, honor, love of liberty, love of country. There are those of us who believe that stimulation of those passions is likewise reasonable.[18]

Lastly, there is the matter of Hamilton's literary style. His style changed and improved over the years, as one might expect (though few scholars seem to have noticed); but what is more significant is that it evolved in a direction. Whatever one thinks of the intellectual merits of his earliest political writings, the 1774-1775 polemics entitled *A Full Vindication of the Measures of Congress* and *The Farmer Refuted*—unlike most other Hamilton scholars, I regard them as extremely muddle-headed—one is struck by their sophomoric literary quality. *The Farmer Refuted*, especially, is studded with strained metaphors, pretentious words, latinisms, citations of authorities (many of whom young Hamilton had obviously not read), and other displays of affected erudition. By 1781-82, when he wrote *The Continentalist* essays, and 1784, when he wrote the *Letters from Phocian*, he had discarded most of that excess baggage, but there was still more than was necessary. By 1788, when he co-authored *The Federalist*, he had almost reached his mature form, but not quite: though he made far fewer classical

---

17. Hamilton's approach to Washington varied, of course, with the situation, the circumstances, and the vicissitudes of the relationship between the two men. For examples, see McDonald, *Hamilton*, 24, 124, 204. 289-296, and the documents cited therein. Both Aly and Arnhart point out that Hamilton's use of ethical proof was essentially as I have described it.

18. Arnhart, "The Federalist as Aristotelian Rhetoric," 25-29; Aly, *Rhetoric of Hamilton*, 142-145, 157-158; Federalist numbers 1, 9, 15, 30 and others. For one of Hamilton's many warnings against emotional or ideological attachments to France, see Pacificus No. IV, July 10, 1793, in Syrett, ed., *Papers of Hamilton*, 15:82-86.

allusions than Madison did, he was still making unnecessary ones, and though he rarely attempted a consciously ornate metaphor, his unconscious metaphors were sometimes mixed or strained. Thereafter, he had arrived: from 1790 until the end of his life his prose style was straightforward, clear, lean, hard, and energetic.[19]

That course of evolution paralleled the growth of Hamilton's commitment to making a success of the American experiment in constitutional government. More than most of his countrymen, he doubted that the experiment could succeed; more than any of them, he was dedicated to making the effort. He perceived clearly that political rhetoric of the highest order was necessary to the attempt, for such is essential to statecraft in a republic. Now, we hear a great deal these days about the public's "right to know." That is a perversion of the truth, even as modern public relations, propaganda, and political blather are perversions of classical rhetoric. If the republic is to survive, the emphasis must be shifted from rights back to obligations. It is the obligation, not the right, of the citizen of a republic to be informed; it is the obligation of the public servant to inform him and simultaneously to raise his standards of judgment. In adapting his style to his audience, Hamilton was fulfilling his part of the obligation.

I would close with a postscript.[20] Despite Hamilton's efforts, and despite the efforts of other patriotic souls, the level of public discourse degenerated rapidly in the late 1790s. A plague of unscrupulous scribblers infested the nation, spewing venom, scurrility, deception, and hysteria throughout the land. Hamilton himself was subjected to as much abuse as any man, and possibly more. But he remained true to his principles until the very end.

One of his last and most celebrated cases as a lawyer arose from the frenzied partisan propaganda warfare that had developed. Harry Croswell, editor of a small-town newspaper, published a report that Jefferson had paid the notorious pamphleteer J. T. Callender to slander Washington, Adams, and other public men. The charge against Jefferson was true; but the Jeffersonians, who had stoutly defended freedom of the press when in the opposition, thought a "few wholesome prosecutions" were in order once they came to power. The Jeffersonian attorney general of New York, Ambrose Spencer, brought proceedings against Croswell for libel. On conviction, he appealed, and Hamilton became his counsel in the arguments before the state supreme court.

The key point at issue was that the judge in the trial court had refused to admit testimony regarding the truth of the statement as defense. English

19. The writings referred to may be found *ibid.*, vols. 1, 4, and 5.
20. Documentation of what follows is to be found in Goebel, ed., *Law Practice of Hamilton*, 1:775-848; the quoted passages are at pages 813, 820-821, and 822.

common-law doctrine, to which Republicans adhered, held that truth was not a defense. Hamilton scored effectively with a bit of emotional proof, showing that the doctrine itself was questionable since it had originated not in common-law courts but in the odious Star Chamber, as a departure from older law. But he was particularly concerned with the suitability of the doctrine in a republic. Libel, he said, was "a slanderous or ridiculous writing, picture or sign, with a malicious or mischievous design or intent, towards government, magistrates, or individuals." Intent was crucial, and truth was relevant to determining intent. Truth was therefore a defense, though not an absolute one. If it were used "wantonly; if for the purpose of disturbing the peace of families; if for relating that which does not appertain to official conduct," it was not acceptable. "But that the truth cannot be material in any respect, is contrary to the nature of things. No tribunal, no codes, no systems can repeal or impair this law of God, for by his eternal laws it is inherent in the nature of things.... It is evident that if you cannot apply this mitigated doctrine for which I speak, to the cases of libels here, you must for ever remain ignorant of what your rulers do. I never can think this ought to be; I never did think the truth was a crime; I am glad the day is come in which it is to be decided; for my soul has ever abhorred the thought, that a free man dared not speak the truth."

# 5

# THE LIBERAL RHETORIC OF FRANKLIN ROOSEVELT

## JOHN ZVESPER

One of the most interesting features of the acceptance speeches of President Carter and Governor Reagan in 1980 was their dispute about who should be able to claim the mantle of Franklin Roosevelt. It is ironic that such a dispute should arise just when Roosevelt's liberalism itself seems to be so out of favor with the American electorate. Of course, Governor Reagan quoted Governor Roosevelt, the Presidential candidate of 1932, who (in agreement with President Hoover) spoke in favor of economy in government — thereby suggesting that the policies of Roosevelt as President did not live up to the candidate's promised thriftiness. But it remains the case that Governor Reagan quoted Franklin Roosevelt and not Hoover. President Carter's response, evasive as it was, nevertheless had a point: "Would you rather quote Herbert Hoover or Franklin Delano Roosevelt?" It would be exaggerated to say that Clinton Rossiter's prediction in 1956 that Roosevelt was "well on his way to enshrinement as a folk hero"[1] has come true, but the little dialogue between President Carter and Governor Reagan did show that Roosevelt's name is still powerful.

A full account of the statecraft and rhetoric of Franklin Roosevelt would consider Roosevelt's leadership of the United States into and through the Second World War. But the most interesting political questions — unhappily not always the most urgent ones — concern the domestic regime, and Roosevelt is rightly remembered primarily not for his leadership in war but for his part in the changes which the New Deal brought to the shape and direction of American politics. The Roosevelt Revolution in party politics, which made the New Deal Democratic Party the center of the American political universe, was not

---

1. *The American Presidency* (2nd edition, New York, 1960), 150.

simply a product of Roosevelt. Drastic changes in the quality of a political
regime can occur because of quantitative changes in the socio-economic basis
of the regime,[2] and it is possible to understand the New Deal as a product of the
growth of a number of interest groups to such prominence that they had to be
given a greater part in the decision-making process of the American regime.
Thus Professor Ladd argues that "the social collectivities, such as urban
workers, so greatly enlarged by industrialization could not have permanently
acquiesced to the supremacy of the entrepreneurs.... The foot soldiers of
industrialism would have demanded that the new economic capacities be used
much more for their benefit even if there had never been a depression...."[3]
However, apart from the fact that industrialization itself can be traced to political causes—to changes of opinion and policy favorable to "industrialism"—it
is important to remember that in politics the way in which a change is understood and the words which are used in public to describe and to acknowledge it
contribute much to its meaning, impact and durability. Roosevelt was the pre-
eminent public spokesman of the New Deal, and this made him a powerful
influence on it. Our question, then, is how well Roosevelt's public definition
and defense of the New Deal met the criteria of healthy liberal democratic
rhetoric.

Political rhetoric can be analysed in a traditional fashion into its three
components: logical elements, basing persuasion on appeals to reason; emotional elements, affecting the passions of the audience; and "ethical" elements,
designed to persuade the audience that the speaker is of sound, trustworthy
character. Assessments of Roosevelt's political skills generally agree that he
excelled at least in the last method of persuasion, partly because his rhetorical
style was relatively lucid and comprehensible. Especially through his use of
radio broadcasts—a medium available to Presidents Coolidge and Hoover but
never as effectively used by them—the vibrant voice of Roosevelt made his
character clearly visible to the public; and he seems to have persuaded significant
numbers of the public that his was a character to be trusted. His chatty style
made him seem one of the people, at the same time that his presidential restraint
in the number and the level of his chats distinguished him from the electronic
demagogues of his day.[4] The ethical element of Roosevelt's rhetoric was so
overwhelming that it is tempting to agree with the judgment that the disparate
programs of the New Deal "were unified only by [his] personality."[5] Roosevelt's

---

2. Aristotle, *Politics* 1302b-1303a.
3. Everett Carll Ladd, Jr., *American Political Parties: Social Change and Political Response* (New York, 1970), 241.
4. Thomas H. Greer, *What Roosevelt Thought* (East Lansing, 1958), 111-112. Roosevelt's fireside chats sometimes quoted lengthy passages from his messages to Congress.
5. Paul Conkin, *The New Deal* (2nd ed., New York, 1975), 1.

successful public relation of his confidence, honesty and ability made him envied and imitated by his successors.

The logical and emotional elements of Roosevelt's rhetoric are more controversial. The New Deal meant public acceptance of the federal government's role as a partner with businessmen, the "princes of property," in the management of the economy.[6] The logic of the New Deal's means of attempting to preserve and to promote a free and prosperous economy is widely questioned today, and has always been questioned by a few. President Coolidge questioned it in advance in his veto of the McNary-Haugen Bill in 1927. Others questioned it more systematically soon after it was put into practice; for example, Walter Lippmann pointed out that New Deal liberalism, in order to avoid dictatorial planning, had to rest satisfied with a "polity of pressure groups," a system of "universal privilege" which has the effect of retarding production because of its monopolistic consequences, even while it incites greater and greater expectations of economic satisfaction in the privileged groups.[7] In defense of the New Deal, one could argue that at least it *has* avoided dictatorial planning, and that the "interest group liberalism" of the United States and other western countries has remained superior economically as well as politically to the eastern scheme of "transmission belt" democracy, in which interest groups are dominated by a revolutionary party's definition of the public interest. One must also wonder whether a scheme more conservative of free markets would have been possible to maintain in the face of the economic disasters of the 1930s. It looks like it will be difficult enough to adopt such a scheme in the relatively more prosperous 1980s. Perhaps the loss of innocence over the last fifty years causes much of this difficulty. But how innocent of monopolistic entanglement was the federal government when Roosevelt became President? How revolutionary in this respect was the New Deal? The great depression—insofar as it was caused by domestic conditions—may well have been caused by conditions opposite to those assumed by New Deal interpretations themselves: not a too *laissez-faire* economy, but an already too heavily politicized, protectionist economy, with a substantial concealed inflation and not too much but too little dynamism in its non-agricultural sectors.[8] Economic historians have not arrived at a definitive answer to this question. Perhaps Roosevelt and his New Deal colleagues were logically misleading when they gave the impression that they knew what to do about the economy (although experience in office sometimes induced in them a little public humility), but their hopeful rhetoric was probably economically helpful

---

6. "Campaign Address on Progressive Government," (Commonwealth Club Address), *Public Papers and Addresses of Franklin D. Roosevelt*, ed. Samuel I. Rosenman (13 vols., New York, 1938-1950), I, 754.

7. *The Good Society* (Boston, 1937), 106-130.

8. Jim Potter, *The American Economy Between the Wars* (London, 1974), 76-89, 92-110.

to the extent that it inspired confidence in the economy and in themselves, and it may have been politically necessary. It is difficult for modern politicians to be economic agnostics. The occasionally skeptical conclusions of economic logic do not easily fit the necessarily confident logic of political rhetoric.

The New Deal also meant that the federal government took the lead in the provision of relief for unemployed workers and welfare benefits for other poor people. Roosevelt justified this as a responsibility which the government had to take upon itself because of the national scope of the problem and because the economic system was failing to provide everyone with the means to actualize his "right to make a comfortable living," a right which Roosevelt deduced from every man's "right to life." He conceded that a man "may by sloth or crime decline to exercise that right; but it may not be denied him." He argued that the political and economic system "owes to everyone an avenue to possess himself of a portion of ["our industrial and agricultural"] plenty sufficient for his needs, through his own work," and that the failure of the economic system to do so meant that the political system had to become more active both as a regulator of business activity and as a provider of relief for the economically "forgotten men."[9] The logic of the welfare state presents problems similar to those of the "polity of pressure groups." The first defense of the logic is also similar. Against the argument that government welfare activity stifles economic incentives and promotes childish dependence on a paternalistic state, one can argue that the social legislation of the New Deal welfare state was a means of forestalling much more revolutionary and illiberal demands.

Perhaps Roosevelt's greater error in the arguments about the economy and public welfare was not the somewhat understandable exaggeration of his omniscience but the misleading exaggeration of the seriousness and depth of these arguments. The New Deal can be defended because it pursued economic rather than spiritual salvation. Roosevelt could claim the not inconsiderable achievement of conserving liberal democratic politics by conserving capitalism, if not as he claimed by removing its "abuses," then at least as he also claimed by preventing the rise to power of those who would try to dispense with free politics and a free economy.[10] But Roosevelt went farther. For example, in a speech at Gettysburg on July 3, 1938, he claimed that the battles of the New Deal were as important and as deep as the battles of the Civil War: "a conflict as fundamental

9. *Public Papers and Addresses*, I, 754; VII, 14.
10. *Public Papers and Addresses*, VII, 10; V, 384-386; "Fireside Chat on Economic Conditions," April 14, 1938, *Nothing to Fear: The Selected Addresses of Franklin Delano Roosevelt, 1932-1945*, ed. B.D. Zevin (London, 1947), 137-138; "Campaign Address at Chicago," October 14, 1936, and "Radio Campaign Address to Business Men," October 23, 1936, *Public Papers and Addresses*, V, 480-489, 534-537; James L. Sundquist, *Dynamics of the Party System* (Washington, D.C., 1973), 197; Arthur A. Ekirch, Jr., *Ideologies and Utopias* (Chicago, 1969), 103 (remarks of Norman Thomas).

as Lincoln's, ... seeking to save for our common country opportunity and security for citizens in a free society."[11] But if economic prosperity is a proper end of liberal politics, it would seem to be so precisely because it draws men's attention and energy away from conflicts "as fundamental as Lincoln's." That is why liberals look primarily not to politics but to private associations for the cultivation of aspiring and inspiring causes. The economic class conflicts which Roosevelt handled, although important and difficult in liberal politics, are in principle less challenging than religious and racial conflicts, because the political establishment of religious and racial differences goes against the grain of liberalism, while economics and economic differences (which can be complementary differences) are useful tools in the liberal political workshop. Perhaps the great depression deserves the gratitude of liberals for focussing American political battles on economic policy rather than on certain other, more inflammatory issues apparent in the 1920s: religion, prohibition, immigration. By transforming the New Deal movement into an evangelical crusade, Roosevelt risked undermining one of that movement's advantages, the fact that it did not pretend to represent final solutions to human problems.

Thomas Silver has contrasted the crusading Roosevelt with the moderate Coolidge, placing Roosevelt among those progressive intellectuals tragically dedicated to committing the American people to an endless series of daring reforms.[12] It is difficult to judge how much Roosevelt was influenced by these "pragmatic" intellectuals. He was an instinctive politician who cultivated people rather than ideas, and this insulated him from the intellectuals; his "brain trust" was in part a way of keeping the intellectuals in their place. Roosevelt was impressed by the extent of change in the circumstances in which the principles of American liberal democracy had to be applied, but he also dimly reflected the understanding of Coolidge and others who, in contrast to progressivism, affirmed the eternal truth of the principles themselves. Roosevelt's definition of human well-being was not constant creativity but the more mundane concerns of material security; it is possible to condemn his political vision for being not too lively and aspiring but too materialistic and deadening. The New Deal tried to alleviate the economic demoralization of the individuals and families who were victims of the depression, but it did not address itself to more spiritual matters; it can therefore be criticized for failing to instill the right kind of morality, but for the same reason it can be defended from the charge that it instilled the wrong kind.

We have also to consider that at least one side of the moral appeal of Roosevelt's New Deal was, in economic terms, not too daring and dynamic, but too timid and static. Roosevelt followed Jefferson and Jackson in expressing

11. *Public Papers and Addresses*, VIII, 419-421.
12. See Thomas Silver, *Coolidge and the Historians*, (Carolina Academic Press, 1983), chapter III.

anxiety about urbanization and industrialization, especially as these adversely affected the economic fortunes of farmers. Thus the great depression, like the economic panics that accompanied critical, realigning elections in the 1790s and the 1830s, occasioned a kind of anticapitalistic conservatism. This conservative anxiety, rather than an innovative liberalism, marked much New Deal rhetoric and policy. Although Roosevelt inherited many of the urban voters for Al Smith, his own background as a Hudson Valley gentleman made it easier for him than it would have been for Smith to indulge farmers visiting the White House with stories about Andrew Jackson's use of the South Grounds for keeping cows and sheep, and with wishes that the White House "could continue to be a farm today."[13] New Deal economic conservatism may have been part of the reason for the shortcomings of New Deal policies which assumed that planned "stabilization" rather than managed dynamism was needed. Roosevelt's best statement of this outlook was his Commonwealth Club Address in San Francisco in September 1932,[14] which begins with a reference to America's "great potentialities of youth," especially in the "great West," but soon moves on to more pessimistic reflections on the need to treat the American economy as a problem in economic geriatrics:

A glance at the situation today only too clearly indicates that equality of opportunity as we have known it no longer exists. Our industrial plant is built; the problem just now is whether under existing conditions it is not overbuilt. Our last frontier has long since been reached, and there is practically no more free land. More than half of our people do not live on the farms or on lands and cannot derive a living by cultivating their own property. There is no safety valve in the form of a Western prairie to which those thrown out of work by the Eastern economic machines can go for a new start. We are not able to invite the immigration from Europe to share our endless plenty. We are now providing a drab living for our people.

This gloomy picture was not an altogether accurate assessment of the state of the economy. For example, there were frontiers open to entrepreneurs in the 1930s in the technological innovations then available but undeveloped until during or after the Second World War. Immigration had declined because of legal barriers, not economic disincentives; this decline was probably more a cause than a symptom of urban economic problems. It was inaccurate observation from which Roosevelt drew his conclusion:

Clearly, all this calls for a re-appraisal of values. A mere builder of more industrial plants, a creator of more railroad systems, an organizer of more

---

13. *Public Papers and Addresses*, IV, 429-432 (October 25, 1935); cf. V, 438 (October 10, 1936). Like Jackson, Roosevelt could see agrarian virtues in certain kinds of businessmen, the "yeomanry of business" (V, 211).

14. *Public Papers and Addresses*, I, 742-756.

corporations, is as likely to be a danger as a help. The day of the great promoter or the financial Titan, to whom we granted anything if only he would build, is over. Our task now is not discovery or exploitation of natural resources, or necessarily producing more goods. It is the soberer, less dramatic business of administering resources and plants already in hand, of seeking to reestablish foreign markets for our surplus production, of meeting the problem of under-consumption, of distributing wealth and products more equitably, of adapting existing economic organizations to the service of the people. The day of enlightened administration has come.

Roosevelt tried to help establish a post-industrial polity which would approximate the conditions of pre-industrial America, where people had been able to "live happily, labor peacefully, and rest secure," without benefit of "the talents of men of tremendous will and tremendous ambition" that had been needed for the industrial revolution. The captains of industry are replaced in this vision by the captains of social work and other enlightened administrators. There were many businessmen who were prepared to go along with such reasoning, because businessmen often did very well out of "enlightened administration." But Roosevelt's call for "a re-appraisal of values" was nevertheless an attack on entrepreneurial business culture, and the New Deal sealed a political alliance of intellectuals and "the people" against "the interests" that had been in the making for some years. One could hope that this alliance would be better from a liberal point of view than an alliance of intellectuals and "the interests," because it seems that it should be weaker. But in fact the attack on business culture persuaded many businessmen that they should restrict themselves — or could get away with restricting themselves — to management and administration, and that the fearful age of dramatic, entrepreneurial daring was past. Liberal critics of the New Deal argue that because the New Deal failed to attack business culture thoroughly enough, it produced in the National Recovery Administration and in other "enlightened administrations" an alliance of big business and big government. Such an alliance was produced by that administration, but the reason it seemed justifiable was not that the business ethic captured the administrators, but that the administrative ethic captivated the businessmen. The problem was not too many entrepreneurial values but too few; not too much daring but too little.

With these qualifications, it remains true that Roosevelt did bring to Washington a more daring activism than President Coolidge had countenanced. In response to criticism from Coolidge's point of view, Roosevelt would be able to reply with the observation that progressive daring is a traditional and essential part of American political practice, as long as it is coupled with moderation and directed by and to the recognition of human equality. This can be seen in Abraham Lincoln's interpretation of the final truths of the Declaration of Independence: "The authors of that notable instrument ... meant to set up a standard maxim for a free society which should be familiar to all: constantly looked to, constantly labored for, and even though never perfectly attained, constantly approximated and thereby constantly spreading and deepening its influence and augmenting the happiness and value of life to all people, of all colors, everywhere."[15] This combination of finality and progress, of moderation and daring, is the problem of liberal democratic rhetoric.

It is undeniable that there were times when Roosevelt neglected the need to couple daring with moderation. One of his most serious mistakes was to encourage the formation of a two-party system based simply on the division between liberalism and conservatism. Having won the elections of 1932 and 1936 by offering a position different from that of the Republicans, Roosevelt resented the Republican moves towards his position and the Democratic moves away from his position in the following years; he tried to purge conservatives from the Democratic party, and to shepherd liberal Republicans into the Democratic fold. The simplification of the American party system in the manner he suggested would have made the coupling of daring and moderation more difficult, either by putting all the daring in one party and all the moderation in the other, or by squeezing moderation out of both parties. The American people were wise to resist Roosevelt's efforts to produce a simple and permanent ideological "system of party responsibility."[16] Ideological divisions and crusades have occasionally proved to be indispensable to American democracy, but it is the rarity and temporary nature of such episodes that has made them acceptable and useful to moderate politicians.

In defense of Roosevelt, it may be observed that the problem of combining daring and moderation is particularly difficult for politicians in liberal democracies. In principle modern liberalism is antipathetic to daring political speech. The philosophical founders of liberalism were much more opposed to the use of rhetoric in politics than previous political philosophers, because rhetoric means passionate controversy which can lead to civil war, and civil war makes insecure the liberal rights to life, liberty, and the pursuit of happiness. Liberal politicians must restrain themselves from using political rhetoric which naturally justifies political ruling, because liberalism intends to avoid the controversies that arise when political ruling—the elevation of one kind of human character over another—is permitted. Liberal politicians hesitate to enlist human passions and spiritedness in the service of their logic, because they reasonably fear that these will bring with them illiberal claims to rule. Yet they must say

15. *The Collected Works of Abraham Lincoln,* ed. Roy P. Basler (9 vols., New Brunswick, 1953-1955), III, 301.
16. *Public Papers and Addresses,* VII, xxvii-xxix; IX, 62-63. In a speech to Republicans in the campaign of 1932, Roosevelt quoted Coolidge on the desirability of an alternation of parties in office, but omitted this from the published version: Greer, *What Roosevelt Thought,* 122-123.

something as strong as these claims, in order to prevent others from being successful in making them. Liberal politicians are bound to engage in politics and rhetoric in spite of themselves. This is true in all liberal regimes, but it is most obvious in liberal democracies, where liberal politicians are obliged to use rhetorical fire not only to fight illiberal flames, but also to create and to maintain the moral warmth of the citizenship and friendship of the democratic community. Although the primary strategy of liberal politics is to depoliticize idealistic moral aspirations and to assist the cultivation of these aspirations in private associations, American political theory and practice have recognized the necessity of cultivating publicly the aspirations of liberal democratic citizenship. This is needed not only to counteract illiberal citizenship, but also to constitute the morality of the regime, and to make possible democratic public opinion as the basis of its policy.

The most important area in which this recognition has appeared in the United States is in laws concerning racial differences. In a dissenting opinion in Plessy v. Ferguson, the famous "separate but equal" case in 1896, Justice Harlan spoke of the "pride of race" which "every true man ... under appropriate circumstances"—that is, in the private sphere—is privileged to express. Here we see the provision for potentially political claims to be cultivated in private, equally separate from political power. But Justice Harlan also suggested a more positive strategy for liberal politicians when he went on to say that liberal government should not "permit the seeds of race hate to be planted under the sanction of law," as in Louisiana's provision of separate railway carriages for different races in the statute upheld by the majority decision in this case. The majority argued that "If one race be inferior to the other socially, the Constitution of the United States cannot put them upon the same plane." Perhaps the majority of the Court were not inaccurate in their assessment of the Court's power to affect racial opinions in 1896. But surely Justice Harlan was correct in his argument that common liberal citizenship is incompatible with a law "which, practically, puts the brand of servitude and degradation upon a large class of our fellow citizens," and which must "create and perpetuate a feeling of distrust between ... races...." A later Court was able to help foster opinions and laws more conducive to the equal dignity of all citizens which is demanded by the logic of liberalism. It is not clear that the reasoning of this Court was as wise as Justice Harlan's and it seems all too clear that the Court today displays even less wisdom in these matters. However, in a footnote to Justice Stevens' partly dissenting opinion in University of California v. Bakke, we can see the same consideration of the importance of replacing "hostility between two great parts of our people" by "a 'meeting of the minds' among all races and a common national purpose."[17]

17. Opinion of Justice Stevens, n. 19, quoting Senator Pastore.

In Roosevelt's first fireside chat of 1936, he spoke in comparable terms about the task for the liberal politician with regard to class difference:

> Tomorrow is Labor Day. Labor Day in this country has never been a class holiday. It has always been a national holiday. It has never had more significance as a national holiday that it has now. In other countries the relationship of employer and employee has been more or less accepted as a class relationship not readily to be broken through. In this country we insist, as an essential of the American way of life, that the employer-employee relationship should be one between freemen and equals. We refuse to regard those who work with hand or brain as different from or inferior to those who live from their property. But our workers with hand and brain deserve more than respect for their labor. They deserve practical protection in the opportunity to use their labor at a return adequate to support them at a decent and constantly rising standard of living, and to accumulate a margin of security against the inevitable vicissitudes of life.
>
> The average man must have that twofold opportunity if we are to avoid the growth of a class-conscious society in this country.
>
> There are those who fail to read both the signs of the times and American history. They would try to refuse the worker any effective power to bargain collectively, to earn a decent livelihood and to acquire security. It is those shortsighted ones, not labor, who threaten this country with that class dissension which in other countries has led to dictatorship and the establishment of fear and hatred as the dominant emotions in human life.[18]

Roosevelt thus interpreted the New Deal for the relatively forgotten Americans as an attempt to help create a democratic community of equal dignity. He thought the social legislation of the New Deal represented a growing sense of "human decency throughout our Nation ... confined to no group or class," an "urge of humanity," which was not "a war of class against class," but "a war against poverty and suffering and ill-health and insecurity, a war in which all classes are joining in the interest of a sound and enduring democracy."[19] He coupled the growth of equal respect among economic classes with the growth of national good will and national loyalties (as opposed to group and sectional loyalties),[20] and linked these to the preservation of liberal democracy and the growth of animate but moderate public opinion:

> There is placed on all of us the duty of self-restraint.... That is the discipline of a democracy. Every patriotic citizen must say to himself or herself, that immoderate statement, appeals to prejudice, the creation of unkindness, are offenses against the whole population of the United States....
> Self-restraint implies restraint by articulate public opinion, trained to distinguish fact from falsehood, trained to believe that bitterness is never a useful instrument in public affairs. There can be no dictatorship by an individual or

18. *Public Papers and Addresses,* V, 338-339.
19. "Acceptance of Third Nomination," *Nothing to Fear,* 220.
20. *Public Papers and Addresses,* V, 149, 213; "Fireside Chat on Legislation," October 12, 1937, *Nothing to Fear,* 118.

by a group in this Nation, save through division fostered by hate. Such division there must never be.[21]

It is not clear that Roosevelt's own rhetoric always lived up to these high standards. He often blamed the depression on the incompetence or sinister designs of the "overprivileged," placing far too much emphasis on high financiers and their irresponsible speculation and distrust of popular control of business and government. In the campaign of 1936, in particular, he may have fostered class hatred and division when, as in his acceptance speech in Philadelphia, he concentrated on the dangers of the "new despotism" of these "economic royalists," whom he compared to the enemies of the Republic in 1776.[22] He was careful sometimes to explain that he did not mean that all financiers were culpable, "any more than Theodore Roosevelt, in using the term 'malefactors of great wealth,' implied that all men of great wealth were 'malefactors.'"[23] Nevertheless he made the accusation in general, class terms, and such general accusations tend to arouse hatred of a class rather than more manageable anger at more punishable individuals.[24] Winston Churchill, in a sketch of Roosevelt written in 1934, called attention to the danger which the temptation to engage in such generalities held for the success of Roosevelt's policies: "It would be a thousand pities if this tremendous effort ... should be vitiated by being mixed up with an ordinary radical programme and a commonplace class fight." Churchill admitted that there was "justification for the anger of the American public against many of their great leaders of finance.... A thousand speeches could be made on this." But he thought the important question was "whether American democracy can clear up scandals and punish improprieties without losing its head, and without injuring the vital impulses of economic enterprise and organisation."[25] Ancient and modern authorities on political rhetoric agree that it should be used to encourage the warm passions which are most in accord with the dictates of cool reason. Liberal democratic rhetoricians who would avoid insipidity but retain moderation must employ not passionate hatred, but merely righteous anger, which is more amenable to reason. The distinction between the two can be difficult, and the "ethical" demands of liberal democratic rhetoric — the necessity of popularity — enlarges the temptation to blur the distinction; but these difficulties are merely signs of the nobility of successful liberal democratic rhetoric. We can conclude that Roosevelt's rhetoric was often but not always successful by these criteria expressed or implied by his own reflections.

21. "Fireside Chat on Economic Conditions," April 14, 1938, *Nothing to Fear,* 142.
22. *Public Papers and Addresses,* V, 230-236.
23. "Campaign Address at Chicago, Illinois," October 14, 1936, *Public Papers and Addresses,* V, 482.
24. Aristotle, *Rhetoric* 1382a; Machiavelli, *Discourses on Livy,* I, 7-8.
25. "Roosevelt from Afar," *Great Contemporaries* (London: Fontana, 1965), 309-311; cf. remarks of Rexford G. Tugwell, "Symposium: Early Days of the New Deal," Morton J. Frisch and Martin Diamond (eds.), *The Thirties: A Reconsideration in the Light of the American Political Tradition* (Northern Illinois University Press, 1968), 129-131.

# 6

# THE DECAY OF PRESIDENTIAL RHETORIC

## JEFFREY TULIS

When President Carter gathered his advisors together at Camp David during the third year of his administration for the so-called "domestic summit," he "channeled the discussions beyond the subjects of energy and economics to the larger question of the nature of the leadership he and his administration [were] providing." The President concluded that he had "fallen into the trap of being head of government," rather than the leader of the people he had promised. As he emerged from Camp David to give his highly publicized "crisis of confidence" speech, the Washington *Post's* front page banner headline proclaimed: CARTER SEEKING ORATORY TO MOVE AN ENTIRE NATION.[1]

This incident serves as a nice vignette of a profound development in twentieth century American politics. Since the presidencies of Theodore Roosevelt and Woodrow Wilson popular or mass rhetoric has become a principal tool of presidential governance and the doctrine that a president ought to be a popular leader has become an unquestioned premise of our political culture. Indeed, far from questioning popular leadership, intellectuals and columnists have embraced the concept and appear to be constantly calling for more or better presidential leadership of popular opinion. Recall again the birth of the Carter "domestic summit." The president had planned to give a nationally televised energy speech, prior to the summit, but called it off, in order to reassess his intention. Throughout the ensuing Camp David meetings public

1. *Washington Post*, July 14, 15, 16, 1979, p. 1.

speculation abounded regarding the competence of Carter's administration, provoked by the mere decision not to give a policy speech.

Near the end of his administration, Carter became the object of a bevy of cartoons and editorials lampooning his "Rose Garden strategy" of making fewer public speeches and appearing preoccupied with "presidential" tasks. No doubt the mirth resulted from Carter's apparent "about face" on popular leadership or from the suspicion that the president was holed up in the Rose Garden engaged in the weighty presidential task of fashioning the series of campaign spots that were to follow. Nevertheless, his motives may properly be distinguished from his professed reasons. These reasons may carry a weight of their own and may be evaluated apart from the circumstances in which they were offered. The argument for the Rose Garden strategy is that the requirements of the office conflict with the requisites of popular speech. It is striking that this argument has not found a sympathetic ear anywhere among our informed public commentators. It is taken for granted today that it is a president's *duty* constantly to defend himself publicly, to promote his policy intiatives nationwide, and to inspirit the population. And for some, this presidential "function" is not one duty among many, but rather the heart of the presidency—its essential task.

While an occasional hiatus in presidential speechmaking causes consternation today, *giving* such speeches was proscribed by the ruling model of presidential leadership, accepted by the public at large, prior to the twentieth century. Before the development of the modern "mass" media, newspaper reporters transcribed *verbatim* the few public presidential addresses and generally included in their renditions heckles and reactions of the audience. Consider the attitude toward popular rhetoric captured a century ago by a newspaperman reporting an address by President-elect Abraham Lincoln.

And here, fellow citizens, I may remark that in every crowd through which I have passed of late some allusion has been made to the present distracted condition of the country. It is naturally expected that I should say something upon this subject, but to touch upon it all would involve an elaborate discussion of a great many questions and circumstances, would require more time than I can at present command, and would perhaps, unnecessarily commit me upon matters which have not yet fully developed themselves. [Immense cheering, and cries of "good!" "that's right!"][2]

Unlike Lincoln, most of the leading students of the Presidency approve of practices labelled here "popular leadership." Yet few of these scholars notice that these constitute a significant change in the conduct of the Presidency. In a recent thorough survey of the contemporary literature on the Presidency, Profes-

---

2. "Speech at Pittsburgh, Pa., February-15, 1861," Roy P. Basler ed. *The Collected Works of Abraham Lincoln*, (9 vols., New Brunswick, NJ: Rutgers University Press) IV, p. 210.

sor Fred Greenstein identifies several features of the contemporary executive thought to be significant departures from the original governmental design.[3] Among these are active initiation and supervision of a legislative program, development of a large White House staff, widespread use of "unilateral" powers (such as executive agreements) and a tendency on the part of the public to hold the president responsible for all of the government's activities. Because all of the alleged changes Professor Greenstein mentions could plausibly be defended with or explained by Hamiltonian principles (and some have been so defended or explained) the supposition that there has been a dramatic "meta-morphosis" of the office seems to be at best a gross exaggeration. Noteworthy for present purposes is the fact that the integration of popular rhetoric into the day to day conduct of the Presidency is *not* mentioned as one of the distinguishing features of the modern Presidency, even though it would be impossible to find a defender of popular leadership among the Founders.

Why was Lincoln's stance, very much a "Rose Garden" position, appre-ciated in his time but not in ours? What was the larger view of the Presidency back of the simple distaste for popular rhetoric? Why did that perspective change? And what have been the political consequences of that change? These are the questions I wish to begin to discuss in this paper. From these introductory remarks, it should be apparent that I wish to rehabilitate the older view. But I should also make clear that I do not intend to build a case for an unequivocal return to the older practice. Practical difficulties as well as kernels of truth embedded in the most sophisticated versions of the contemporary dogma pre-vent our re-living the past. Outlining the development of the rhetorical Pres-idency will highlight some dilemmas inherent in a republican executive.

It may seem strange to some, (particularly those whose profession it is to study early American political history or modern political philosophy) that I state so adamantly the Founders' opposition to popular rhetoric because the theme of rhetoric does not stand out among the topics discussed by the Founders or by their great modern philosophical tutors.[4] Perhaps the reason for the low priority of rhetoric as an outstanding theme for the Founders is also a clue to their understanding of the proper function of political rhetoric. To put the matter

3. Fred Greenstein, "Change and Continuity in the American Presidency," in Anthony King, ed. *The New American Political System* (Washington, DC: American Enterprise Institute, 1978).
4. Of course, Hobbes was greatly influenced by Aristotle's *Rhetoric*. And Marx translated the *Rhetoric*, but both appear to have been intrigued by the political understanding of the work and of the analysis of the passions in particular rather than in the surface intention to teach an art of rhetoric. See Leo Strauss, *The Political Philosophy of Hobbes*, (Chicago: University of Chicago Press, 1952) and Karl Marx, "Letter to His Father: On a Turning Point in His Life (1837)" in Loyd D. Eason and Kurt H. Guddet, *Writings of Young Marx on Philosophy and Society* (New York: Doubleday & Co., 1967), p. 47

crudely, the lowering of the comprehensive political objectives from antiquity to modernity—from the inculcation of virtue to the establishment of security and the protection of rights—brought with it a change in understanding of how to deal with the problems posed by political rhetoric and a narrowing of the tasks of rhetoric. No longer responsible for elevating the soul, rhetoric could be confined and enlisted to support *institutions* whose purpose it was to maintain security and to protect rights.

For the Founders, men would be governed by *institutions* (as it is often said, institutions with teeth in them) and only indirectly by *doctrine*, which forms those institutions. The problems of political rhetoric, they hoped, would be controlled by the working of those institutions. Thus, it is in their discussion of the major national institutions that the Founders addressed the questions of rhetoric, although often not employing the term "rhetoric" when discussing it. The Founders' rhetoric on rhetoric is not primarily addressed to rhetoricians, but to institution builders and to people who would live under the rule of those institutions. To the extent that the Founders' rhetoric addressed potential rhetoricians, it did not offer a teaching of an art of rhetoric but rather a teaching on "institutional maintenance." For ambitious Americans, fame could be won in and through institutions with a rhetoric appropriate to those institutions.

The closest the Founders came to discussing rhetoric directly was in their discussions of demagoguery, which, as James Ceaser has noted, begin and end *The Federalist*.[5] Yet even here the issue is addressed primarily in an institutional context. True, the citizenry is warned away from wily politicians who disagree with *The Federalist* on the merits of the proposed Constitution, but the most informative discussions occur in the course of consideration of the structure of the legislature and of the executive.

With respect to the structure of the major political branches, two concerns are particularly germane to our topic—separation of powers and independence of the executive. It is common today among political scientists studying the Presidency to view these conceptions as inadequate explanations of the actual functioning of presidential power, or misguided "normative" stances. Richard Neustadt, for example, suggests that rather than "separation of powers" we in fact live under "separate institutions sharing power."[6] In back of Neustadt's suggestion is the premise that power is an undifferentiated lump—a single kind of thing—which was divided in order to prevent any one branch from exercising tyranny over the others. This view finds some support in the founding deliber-

5. For the best available analysis of the Founders' understanding of the problems of demogoguery see, James W. Ceaser, *Presidential Selection: Theory and Development*, (Princeton, NJ: Princeton University Press, 1979).
6. Richard Neustadt, *Presidential Power* new ed., (New York: John Wiley & Sons, 1980) p. 26, 28-30, 170, 176, 204.

ations. Much consideration was given to making each branch "weighty" enough to resist encroachments by the others. Yet this "checks and balances" view can better be understood as subservient to an alternative understanding of separation of powers expressed throughout the founding period. Powers were to be separated because each branch would be best equipped to do *different* tasks. Separation of powers is thus understood as separation of functions, with institutions constructed to serve those functions best. Each branch would be superior in its own sphere and in its own way.[7] Many have noted how and why legislative, executive, and judicial power differ, or why deliberation is the desired quality of legislatures while decisiveness is the needed function of executives. But what is not often noticed is that many of the "checks and balances" provisions can be understood not only as attempts to prevent encroachment but also as devices to improve further those central functions. For example, the qualified veto not only prevents "unconstitutional" legislation, it improves deliberation by extending the process and broadening the relevant considerations.

It could be hoped that public policy considerations would be broadened by drawing the president into the legislative process through the veto or the prospect of a veto because the president would bring to the legislation a different *perspective* from Congress. Like separation of powers, the independence of the executive not only afforded the president security from "encroachment" or control by the legislature, it had a positive purpose as well. Independence of the executive (achieved primarily through constitutional grants of authority and a nonlegislative, nonpopular mode of election) permitted the president to view the whole as no one else in or out of the government could view it. Noteworthy, of course, is the fact that "independence" was freedom from continual, day to day, direct popular influence, as well as congressional influence.

Attached to the presidential *privilege* of a veto is a *duty* to present Congress with a veto message stating "his objections to that House in which the bill shall have originated, who shall enter the objections at large on their Journal, and proceed to reconsider it."[8] Presidential rhetoric is mentioned one other time in the Constitution: "He shall from time to time give to the Congress Information of the State of the Union, and recommend to their Consideration such Measures as he shall judge necessary and expedient."[9] In each instance, the president is directed to address Congress, not the people at large. Presidential rhetoric would thus be public, though not popular. And while it could be presumed that presidents would occasionally address the people through Congress, the indirect route does place a "deliberative" constraint on rhetoric. The stipulated

7. In addition to the well known discussions in the Federal convention and in *The Federalist*, the *Annals of Congress*, Gales ed., (1834), Vol. 1, 0. 384-412; 476-608.
8. Constitution, Art. 1, Sec. 7.
9. Constitution, Art. 11, Sec. 3.

addressee cannot simply be ignored and the format is primarily a written one.[10] (Rarely in the 19th century did presidents appear personally before Congress for any purpose.)[11]

The Inaugural Address is the only "official" popular address that extends throughout our history. Contrary to common understanding, it is not mentioned or implied by any of the clauses of the Constitution, but its early adoption was made consistent with the spirit of the principles outlined above. Glen Thurow has noted that early 19th century Inaugural Addresses can generally be described as attempts to articulate the principles of republican government.[12] The interpretations of republicanism offered had an important bearing on the mode and substance of policies proffered later in the administration but no particular plans were articulated or visions unfolded as they are in contemporary Inaugural Addresses. Later in the 19th century, the general policies of the incoming administration were alluded to in the addresses foreshadowing contemporary practice. But even in these late 19th century speeches, Thurow notes, the principal aim was to show how a new general direction of policy was consistent with republicanism, not to discuss the merits of a proposed legislative program. None of the 19th century presidents attempted (as do current presidents-elect) to build "visions" of the future out of undisciplined vulgarizations of leading strands of contemporary thought. Nineteenth century presidents were disciplined by the accepted practice of having to square one's vision with the Constitution.

Messages to Congress and the Inaugural Address constituted most of "official" presidential rhetoric in the 19th century. Occasional ceremonial addresses (Washington's Birthday, for example) and "Proclamations" completed the 19th century "official" corpus. I have discovered a sizable body of "unofficial" presidential speeches addressed to groups of ordinary citizens. The fact that this material is hard to find today is itself an indication of the intended place of popular rhetoric in the conduct of the Presidency. Most had little direct influence on public policy and were soon forgotten. (A conspicuous exception is Lincoln's

10. And these formed messages constituted a body of precedent, something of a common law of rhetoric, often consulted when a president began to constitute his message. See especially, Rutherford B. Hayes, *Diary of a President* (publication data unavailable) and Edwin Williams, ed., *Statesman's Manual* (2 vols, New York: Edward Walker, 1849).
11. Washington began the practice of delivering the Annual Message or (State of the Union Message) in person before a joint session of Congress. The practice was abandoned by Jefferson and remained dormant until Woodrow Wilson re-instituted it. An important element of the original practice *not* reinstituted by Wilson was the written "reply" of Congress that followed a week or two of deliberation on the presidential address. See, Daniel Webster, "The Presidential Protest," Speech delivered in the Senate, May 7, 1834, *Works* (6th ed. 1853) Vol. IV, p. 108ff. which reflects back upon the rhetoric of "reply."
12. Glen E. Thurow, "Voice of the People: Speechmaking and the Modern Presidency," An Address Delivered at Wake Forest University, October 1, 1979.

Gettysburg Address.) To locate these speeches, most of which occurred on "tours" to various regions of the nation, one must exhume contemporary biographies, local newspapers, and occasional 19th century private compilations. The first tour was taken by Washington and the form of his speeches set the tone for most that were to follow. Washington used the occasions to remind the people of republican principles and to rekindle patriotic sentiments. Monroe and others later in the century followed the practice but sometimes added the objective of establishing "harmony" between the regions of the nation and contained discussions of policy similar to those found in the late nineteenth century Inaugural Addresses.[13]

There is one important exception to the general characterization of pre-twentieth century presidential rhetoric, but it is an exception that supports the general view. President Andrew Johnson, *against the advice* of most of his counselors frequently gave speeches to randomly assembled groups—occasionally to mobs. In 1866, he embarked on a presidential tour, though fittingly he renamed the excursion "The Swing Around the Circle." The tour differed markedly from all previous tours. But in its unfettered use of popular rhetoric in support of particular policy initiatives before Congress it foreshadowed (indeed, serves as a fine caricature of) twentieth century presidential tours. It is worth noting that Teddy and Franklin Roosevelt labelled their tours on behalf of legislation "Swings Around the Circle."

"On Monday, February the 24th, 1868, The House of Representatives of the Congress of the United Stated resolved to impeach Andrew Johnson, President of the United States, of high crimes and misdemeanors, of which, The Senate was apprised and arrangements were made for the trial."

Little known and long forgotten is the fact that the 10th Article of Impeachment was for the bad rhetoric expressed on the "Swing Around the Circle" and in other speeches. "That said Andrew Johnson, President of the United States, unmindful of the high duties of his office and the dignity and propriety thereof ... did ... make and deliver with a loud voice certain intemperate, inflammatory, and scandalous harangues, and did therein utter loud threats and bitter menaces as well against Congress as the laws of the United States...."[14] The impeachment charge of bad and improper rhetoric has been forgotten probably for three reasons: first, the Tenure of Office Act issue was the basis for ten of the eleven articles; second, many Congressmen participating in the impeachment process were skeptical that "bad rhetoric" constituted an impeachable offense; and finally, due to the unreflective acceptance of popular leadership in our time, the

13. See for example, J. Putnam Waldo, *The Tour of James Monroe, President of the United States, Through the Northern and Eastern States in 1817*, Second ed. (Hartford: Silas Andras, 1820), pp. 149-83.

14. See *Proceedings in the Trial of Andrew Johnson*, 1869, p. 1, 5-6.

few scholars who have noted the charge assumed it must have been "frivolous."[15]

But the significant fact is that no Congressman expressly disagreed with the opinion that Johnson's rhetoric was improper. And of those Congressmen who were reluctant to press the charge, most based their opinion on *strategic* considerations (whether the defense could delay the trial) rather than upon the judgement that the charge was improper.

The major proponent of the charge was one General Butler, a man whose past hindered the sober consideration of his arguments. Butler was a famous public speaker known for bursts of demagoguery. Yet Butler rightly pointed out that impeachment could *better* be defended on the grounds of public harangues than on violation of the Tenure of Office Act—a technical charge that ran counter to the resolution of most removal controversies of the past. Said Butler:

> "... we have only presented to the Senate and country the bones and sinews of the offenses of Andrew Johnson. I want to clothe those naked bones and sinews with flesh, enliven them with blood, and show him as he is, the living, quivering sinner that he is, before this country. Why, Sir, hereafter, when posterity shall come to examine the proceedings of this day, if they need only the articles which have heretofore been presented covering the Tenure of Office Act, they will wonder why, even with so good a case as we have upon mere questions of technical law, we undertook, without other provocation, to bring this prosecution against a good and great man, as The President, without other proof or allegation, might be presumed to have been."[16]

Butler rested his case on precedents drawn from impeachments of sitting judges (Chase and Humphreys) accused of making inflammatory harangues. It was objected that while the judges made their "harangues" from the bench, in their "official" capacities, Johnson made his on tour and in unofficial, off-the-cuff, remarks. Butler rightly responded: "But a judge exercises his office only while on the bench, while The President of the United States can always exercise his office, can exercise it wherever he may be. He can never divest himself of his high character."

The president never goes "on recess;" his residence is his official "office" (The White House or the "Western" White House, etc.) because the chief executive is in an official capacity all of the time. It could only be expected that the distinction between "official" and "popular" speech could not be maintained.

Today a president has an assembly line of speechwriters officially producing words that enable him to say something on every conceivable occasion.

15. See for example, Louis Fisher, *The Constitution Between Friends, Congress, the President, and the Law.* (New York: St. Martin's Press, 1978), p. 154.
16. *Congressional Globe,* March 3, 1868, 40th Cong. 2nd Sess. p. 1640.

Generally, these speechwriters are "wordsmiths" divorced from the policymaking staffs, although their choice of words sometimes affects policy. Advertising agencies—or their executives—and pollsters play a significant role in the construction of the major public addresses. A day scarcely goes by without at least one major news story devoted to coverage of a radio or TV speech, an address to Congress, or some other presidential utterance. Just a glance at the *Public Papers of The President* is enough to indicate the enormous growth of "official" rhetoric. And a perusal of the major speeches themselves is enough to indicate the precipitous decline in quality of argumentation. Indeed, many speeches can aptly be described as having no argument at all.

These facts are known to many even among those who champion popular leadership. The standard reponse to them is a call for better rhetoricians—men or women who will, by virtue of their skills, give better speeches. Other more sophisticated analysts trace the problem to the political context in which any president (however skillful) will find himself. Television and radio, the breakdown of parties and the concomitant lengthening of political campaigns, and the institutionalization of a speechwriting staff within the White House constitute the most important elements of the "political context."

To be sure, these factors are extremely important and would have to be addressed in any comprehensive treatment of presidential rhetoric. Each has an influence on rhetoric traceable to characteristics peculiar to it. For example, television news, with its thirty second segment format, creates an incentive for presidents to build speeches out of one sentence paragraphs (often with no overall development or sequence). With single sentence paragraphs, the president can count on getting a snappy quotation on TV or can count on *not* being quoted out of context, because there is no context.[18]

Rather than canvass these contemporary factors in the political environment, I want to explore the more basic doctrine that is unwittingly accepted by many of those who criticize the media, the primary system, or the White House staff. The "doctrine" is simply the set of arguments that surround and support the opinion that a president ought to be a popular leader. Without this basic opinion, the current uses of TV, the changes in presidential campaigns, and the development of a speechwriting operation would not be regarded as legitimate.

The modern doctrine of presidential leadership was consciously formulated and put into practice by Woodrow Wilson. Explicitly attacking the Founders' understanding of the structure of American politics, Wilson offered a systemic view which culminated in a call for vigorous and continual popular leadership of public opinion. Wilson suggested that "separation of powers" simply did not

17. *Ibid.* p. 1641.
18. Interview, James Fallows (former head speechwriter, Carter Administration). March 1, 1979. White House "politics" and the organizational dynamics involved in constructing a speech also contribute to the disjointed character of most presidential addresses today.

work. He contended that American politics had been characterized by stalemate between the branches. Since each branch had too much power over the others, little legislation was formed and implemented. This argument foreshadowed many of the arguments in the 1950's for party reform. As Walter Berns has pointed out, the party reform argument that the system needed to be changed to make the federal government more active ignored the fact that it was the political disposition of President Eisenhower, not the system, which was responsible for the lack of policies that the reformers preferred.[19] Similarly, Wilson attributed the lack of his preferred Progressive legislation to a defect in the *system*—the lack of a single source of leadership. After experimenting with the thought that leadership could come from within the legislature, Wilson settled on the Presidency as the source of new energy for the system. The president's connection to the people could be exploited to give him more weight with respect to Congress. Whereas in the older practice presidents spoke to the people through Congress, in Wilson's scheme the president would speak to Congress via his speeches to the people.[20]

While one theme of Wilson's reinterpetation of the American system was the need for a more active and effective government, another was the need for better civic education. Compared to contemporary populists, Wilson had a somewhat complex view of the relation of the leader to the people. On the one hand, the leader was to draw his ideas, his program, and his vision from the people. On the other hand, such ideas would generally be *unknown* to the people until Wilson articulated them. The people would express various desires and interests but it would require a leader to make their meaning manifest. One may rightly wonder whether this aristocratic insight could fail to be vulgarized, packaged as it was in a democratic teaching. In any event, it added a dimension to Wilson's argument that eventually culminated in FDR's claim that the president was the "moral trumpet" of the nation, and it pointed to a legitimate defect in a system biased against popular rhetoric.

The Wilsonian reinterpretation replaced "separation of powers" with a system absolutely dependent on the executive and replaced the notion of a "privileged position" due to presidential "independence" with a privileged mandate based upon an intimate connection to the people. Finally, Wilson was less concerned with the problem of demagoguery than were the Founders. Replacing "institutions" as a control on the wily politician would be the good sense of the people. This faith in the "enlightenment" of the people, while obviously

19. Walter Berns, "Reform of the American Party System," in Robert Goldwin, ed. *Political Parties, U.S.A.* (Chicago: Rand McNally, 1964), p. 56.
20. For Wilson's understanding of presidential leadership see, *Constitutional Government in the United States* (New York: Columbia University Press, 1908); *Leaders of Men*, ed. T.H. Vail Matter (Princeton, NJ: Princeton University Press, 1952) and see also Ceaser, *Presidential Selection*, Chapter 4 for a discussion of different themes.

problematic should not be simply dismissed. Consider, for example, the public reaction to Carter's campaign claim that should his opponent be elected the nation would be divided—ethnically, regionally, rich from poor, etc. The public reaction suggests the possibility that the people may indeed be good judges of some forms of demagoguery, although not all (such as the soft flattery that used to characterize Carter's speeches and now appears the thrust of Reagan's).

Wilson offered a "reinterpretation" of American politics that could not simply replace the old view—based as the old view was on actual institutions, not just opinion. The Founders' institutions and through them their principles continue to "mold" the Presidency: presidents continue to *act* occasionally as the Founders intended. As Herbert Storing suggested in another context, American presidents ocasionally "do" statesmanship "in the broader and more traditional sense, but they do not understand it. Therefore, they often do not do it very well."[21] Indeed, the present situation of uneasy coexistence of the old institutions and the modern dogma has generated several serious problems:

1)"Credibility gaps" which are frequently attributed to the character of presidents may also be traced to the competing imperatives of the old and new models of presidential rhetoric. For example, when Woodrow Wilson took his case for the League of Nations "over the heads of Congress" to the people, he was forced to make different arguments to "the people" than to the Senate. To the Senate committee he emphasized the fragility of the enterprise, the difficulties of making it succeed, and the need for the United States to get the League going; to the people, he suggested, we would be left behind and left out if we did not immediately ratify an agreement which the whole world knew to be right.[22] Recent presidents have made different cases to Congress and to the people in the areas of energy policy. To Congress, the standard argument has been the need for a long range policy *to avoid* an energy crisis; to the people, a different rhetorical imperative prevails—presidents find they have to argue that a crisis already *exists*, to build their case for immediate action.[23]

2) Occasionally, the deliberations of Congress serve as a competing or conflicting source of public argument, but are themselves affected by talk to the popular audience. In short, deliberation breaks down. Presidential rhetoric to the people sets the agenda for Congressional discussion. Such seems to have been the case in several of the "Great Society" programs such as the War on Poverty.

21. Herbert Storing, "American Statesmanship: Old and New," in Robert Goldwin, ed. *Bureaucrats, Policy Analysts, Statesmen: Who Leads?* (Washington, DC: American Enterprise Institute, 1980) p. 89.

22. I have discussed the rhetoric of Wilson's League fight in "Thought, Speech, and Deed: On studying Presidential Rhetoric," Paper delivered at 1978 Annual Meeting of American Political Science Association as part of Foundations of Political Theory Group panels.

23. Sanford Weiner and Aaron Wildausky, "The Prophylactic Presidency," *The Public Interest*, Summer 1978.

3) Presidents who are *not* themselves masterful orators—in total control of their persuasive attempts—may begin *to think* in terms of popular speech. Instead of being a watered down version of a complex issue tailored for a popular audience, popular rhetoric may begin to form the president's understanding.

To be sure, the use of popular rhetoric by presidents has brought some positive benefits as well. Teddy Roosevelt's Swing Around the Circle campaigning for the Hepburn Act can be viewed as a *moderating* influence on the demagoguery then prevalent in Congress, and similarly Franklin Roosevelt's "Swing" on behalf of the Social Security Act was designed to moderate the debate between "Socialists" and "Libertarians."[24] Finally, the need to use popular rhetoric in times of war can quite obviously be defended. The difficulty is one of ensuring the benefits and avoiding the defects of popular rhetoric by *institutional means*. How does one provide for institutions or establish a general practice that ensures a day to day conduct free from rhetorical excess, but positively encourages high-minded rhetoric in times of crisis? And how does one encourage high-minded rhetoric in times of crisis without such rhetoric then becoming the norm for day to day politics? I have come to believe that this dilemma is only partly solvable—that while the day to day conduct of our government may be regulated by institutions and practices established by reflection and choice, for extraordinary rhetoric we are "forever destined to depend ... on accident."[25]

24. Elmer Cornwell, *Presidential Leadership of Public Opinion*, (Bloomington, Ind.: Indiana University Press, 1964).
25. *The Federalist*, No. 1.

# 7

# COOLIDGE AND THE RHETORIC OF THE REVOLUTION

## THOMAS B. SILVER

Many liberal and conservative intellectuals are reaching an ominous consensus about the character of the American political order. They are coming to agree that America is Lockean. Lockean means: capitalistic, bourgeois, materialistic, devoid of the higher virtues, acquisitive, crassly self-indulgent. Understood in this way, America at its best is a kind of Falstaff—harmless, fat, and tolerant. It may be unlovely and unlovable, or even repulsive; it is not tyrannical. It has not, like the ideological visionaries of our century, drenched the earth in blood in pursuit of utopian ideals. As Professor Martin Diamond once said, by way of defending the American regime against its critics, "If it fails to measure up to the claims of virtue, that regime may at least be easily defended from the spurious claims of idealism."

Nevertheless, liberals and conservatives are not content to leave the matter there. To say that a man is not a murderer is hardly to excuse his being a glutton, a lecher, or a drunk. What is wanted is repentance and reform. In cases of advanced dissolution, the inspiration for repentance and reform must come, as it were, from without. Liberals seek that inspiration in a vision of the future; conservatives seek it in the authority of the past. Neither seeks inspiration in the principles of the American regime itself, as expressed, for example, in the Declaration of Independence. The American founding was a Lockean founding, and the Declaration of Independence is a Lockean document.

The alpha and the omega of liberalism are identical to the alpha and the omega of Marxism. The alpha is the class struggle and the omega is the termination of the class struggle in the universal, classless society. For Marxists the link between the alpha and the omega is violent revolution; for liberals it is social democracy or some variant. Liberals believe that the class struggle can be softened and carried on within the framework of the democratic principles of the Declaration. But liberals do not claim to find in the Declaration (except perhaps through a creative reinterpretation of it) the ideal for which the class struggle is fought, namely, economic equality. For liberals the present political task is to supplement the political democracy of the Declaration with economic democracy.

For many conservatives, as for many liberals, the Declaration of Independence is defective precisely because it is a Lockean document. It sanctions a society in which the protection of property rights and of unfettered acquisitiveness is second to nothing. From the point of view of liberals, unfettered acquisitiveness leads sooner or later to vast disparities of wealth and economic power and thus to economic oppression. Conservatives are alarmed because the Declaration, by leaving individuals free to pursue unlimited money-making and pleasure, frees them at the same time from moral and religious restraints and obligations.

Now of course, John Locke did not boldly announce his intention to undermine virtue and religion in the name of commerce. According to an interpretation of Locke's thought that is fashionable among some conservatives, this was his secret or esoteric intention, which he concealed beneath a cautious rhetoric. This secret intention was smuggled into the American founding by Locke's disciples among the Founding Fathers. As Professor Diamond said in a speech to which we have already referred, the work of the Founding Fathers was intended to "magnify and multiply the effects of the selfish, the interested, the narrow, the particular, the economic. That is the stratum on which our political system was intended to rest and that is where it rests still. And that is the source of what is vulgar, commercial, and materialistic in our system."

Over time Locke's esoteric principles were to insinuate their way into the soul of Americans and corrode those cultural and religious opinions which had previously been thought to be the supports of decent political life but which in Locke's view were impediments to human progress. To the extent that this has happened, American history may be seen as the unfolding of the latent promise of Locke's teaching: wealth beyond the dreams of avarice. And American capitalism may be seen as a juggernaut, crushing any sense of community, of the common good, of idealism, of divine presence, of human nobility.

Historians generally regard the 1920's as the culmination of America's Lockean history.

The decade of the twenties was dull, bourgeois, and ruthless. 'The business of America is business,' said President Calvin Coolidge succinctly, and the observation was apt if not profound. Wearied by idealism and disillusioned about the war and its aftermath, Americans dedicated themselves with unashamed enthusiasm to making and spending money. Never before, not even in the Mckinley era, had American society been so materialistic, never before so completely dominated by the ideal of the marketplace or the techniques of machinery.[1]

The president of the United States during the twenties was Calvin Coolidge. If America is the most materialistic nation on earth, and if the twenties were the most materialistic decade in American history, Calvin Coolidge is thought to be the perfect symbol and celebrant of America at its worst. Locke's esoteric teaching having insinuated its way into the souls of Americans, there was no longer any need to keep up Locke's rhetorical facade. In all the history books Coolidge is portrayed as the man who regarded acquisitiveness not as an evil or even a necessary evil, but as a positive good; who regarded money-making not as base but as noble; who in a word exalted the Almighty Dollar.

William Allen White, who knew him well, called him a mystic, a whirling dervish of business, as persuaded of the divine character of wealth as Lincoln had been of the divine character of man, 'crazy about it, sincerely, genuinely, terribly crazy.'[2]

Despite the noble words and the lofty hope, to many the New Era seemed at heart only a stampede to make money....

And so it seemed: the single motive had been nurtured until it drove out all others. Joseph Eastman, a distinguished Wilson appointment to the Interstate Commerce Commission, protested against the prevalent philosophy. The pursuit of private gain did not seem to him, he said, as it evidently did to Coolidge, *'the only impelling force in human beings' which could produce desirable results.*[3]

But one can be a mystic, indeed one can be as fanatic as a dervish or a dreamer and still believe in the mysticism which justifies business *for its own sake.* Coolidge exalts the ideals of the peddler, the horse trader, the captain of industry.[4] (emphasis mine)

Of course, historians of the twenties always offer up aphorisms from Coolidge's speeches to prove how simple-minded and crass he really was. For instance, William Leuchtenburg, a prominent historian of the twenties, in his

---

1. Henry Steele Commager and Allan Nevins, *A Pocket History of the United States* (New York: Pocket Books, 1976), p. 410.
2. Arthur M. Schlesinger, Jr., *The Crisis of the Old Order* (Boston: Houghton Mifflin Company, 1957), p. 57.
3. Ibid., pp. 74-75.
4. William Allen White, *Calvin Coolidge: The Man Who is President* (New York: The MacMillan Company, 1925), p. 218.

book *The Perils of Prosperity*, quotes Coolidge as saying, "Brains are wealth, and wealth is the chief end of man."

In Book X of the *Ethics* Aristotle mentions Eudoxus, a man who believed that pleasure is the good. "Eudoxus' arguments," says Aristotle, "gained credence more because of his excellent character than on their own merit. As he had the reputation of being a man of unusual self-control, people thought that he was propounding his theories not because he was addicted to pleasure, but because what he said was acutally true." Such is the common view of Calvin Coolidge, the Puritan in Babylon. Coolidge, a man of unusual self-control, was the moral symbol the times seemed to demand, because his rhetoric sanctified an unholy age and his character made his rhetoric persuasive.

"Brains are wealth, and wealth is the chief end of man." One of the unfortunate things about the history book in which this quotation appears is that it has no footnotes. My own knowledge of Coolidge's works is not exhaustive, but it is extensive, and I have never run across this sentence or any sentiment similar to the one expressed therein. On the contrary, I have come across many explicit assertions to the contrary in Coolidge's speeches and writings. For example, speaking before a group of businessmen in 1916, Coolidge deplored that under the influence of prosperity, "men came to think that *prosperity was the chief end of man* and grew arrogant in the use of its power." (Emphasis mine)

In what must be his best remembered and most frequently misquoted aphorism, Coolidge once said that "The chief business of the American people is business." In this he was surely right: America is in fact a commercial republic. But he then went on to argue that wealth is to be feared when it becomes an end rather than a means.

Wealth is the product of industry, ambition, character and untiring effort. In all experience, the accumulation of wealth means the multiplication of schools, the increase of knowledge, the dissemination of intelligence, the encouragement of science, the broadening of outlook, the expansion of liberties, the widening of culture. Of course, the accumulation of wealth cannot be justified as the chief end of existence. *But we are compelled to recognize it as a means to well-nigh every desirable achievement. So long as wealth is made the means and not the end, we need not greatly fear it.*[5]

Here of course Coolidge is making the commonsensical and traditional argument according to which external goods and goods of the body are elements of

5. Calvin Coolidge, *Foundations of The Republic* (Freeport: Books for Libraries Press, 1926), pp. 187-188.

happiness but are ultimately subordinate to, or for the sake of, the goods of the soul, e.g., "knowledge," "intelligence," "science," "culture." ("Many actions can only be performed with the help of instruments, as it were: friends, wealth, political power."[6])

"Brains are wealth, and wealth is the chief end of man." It is safe to conjecture that this quotation, if it could be found in Coolidge's writings, would be hedged about with the appropriate qualifiers or would mean in context something other than it means out of context. But let us for the moment pursue the scholarship of Professor Leuchtenburg a bit further. *The Perils of Prosperity*, although it does not have footnotes, does have a bibliography. In that bibliography, Professor Leuchtenburg cites an essay written by the novelist Irving Stone. Upon reading that essay, which is a savage attack on President Coolidge (at whose doorstep we must lay not only the Great Depression but also Hitler and World War Two), one discovers that it is the work of a mean-spirited partisan hack. It is replete with factual errors, misquotations, and misrepresentations. Nevertheless, here we do indeed find Coolidge saying, "Brains are wealth, and wealth is the chief end of man." Now, why a reputable professional historian went to an unreliable and vicious hack to research Coolidge's political thought, instead of simply opening up a book of Coolidge's speeches (none of which appears in Leuchtenburg's bibliography), is not a question to detain us at this moment. We are interested in tracing the quotation. Unfortunately, though not surprisingly, Stone's essay does not have footnotes either. However, it is evident that Stone's essay relies for much of its raw material on William Allen White's famous biography of Coolidge, *A Puritan in Babylon*. A careful re-reading of that book would at last bring us to page 253, where we would find the sentence, brains are wealth and wealth is the chief end of man. *But White makes no pretense of quoting Coolidge.* The words are *White's*, though he attributes the sentiment to Coolidge. (It is interesting that White, in the very passage where he attributes to Coolidge the belief that wealth is the chief end of man, quotes Coolidge's aphorism that the business of America is buisness but does not quote from later in the same address where Coolidge says that wealth is not the chief end of existence.)

What seems to have happened then is this: William Allen White attributed to Calvin Coolidge a belief that Coolidge had repeatedly rejected in his speeches and writings. Ten years later the sentence was picked up by a rabid partisan, who put quotation marks around it. Ten years after that a leading historian put the sentence into a popular history, without checking its authenticity, and there it became for thousands of students and readers a sample of Coolidge's thoughts on the purpose of human existence.

6. Aristotle, *Ethics*, Book I.

The central theme of the rhetoric of Calvin Coolidge, the thread that runs through all of his public speeches and writings, is not the exaltation of greed but the exhortation to virtue. In his book, *The Crisis of the Old Order,* Professor Arthur Schlesinger Jr. says that in Coolidge's time, "The concept of 'character' was basic in the morality of conservatism." He then launches into a biting attack on the hypocrisy of the leading conservatives, showing how various of them "contributed to their own degradation." Coolidge himself Schlesinger begins by calling "a fanatic for the old-fashioned virtues," and he concludes by implying that Coolidge's "character" was actually "a bankruptcy of mind and soul." However that may be, Schlesinger has surely put his finger on the central difference between conservatives and radicals. The former, believing that human progress and happiness depend upon character, know "that evil cannot be eradicated and therefore that one's expectations from politics must be moderate." The latter, believing that human progress and happiness depend not upon the disciplining but upon the liberation of the passions, know that one's expectations from politics must be great. Freedom is infinitely easier to achieve than virtue.[7]

This fundamental difference between conservatives and radicals will find expression in two sharply opposed rhetorics. Radicals, seeing that the world could "easily" be so much better than it is, feel a sense of urgency about transforming the human condition, and they attempt in their rhetoric to convey this sense of urgency to the people. But as all intelligent radicals know, the people are for many reasons inherently conservative. By definition the many cannot be ahead of their times. For this reason it is the duty of the intellectuals through their rhetoric to inspire the people with a vision of the future and to instill in them a radical dissatisfaction with the status quo. The status quo is contemptible in contrast to the shining future that will arrive just as soon as the people will their own liberation. The citizens therefore must be schooled in self-contempt.

Conservatives know that good character is the product of good laws and good institutions. Good character is the end and good laws and institutions are the means to it. Conservative rhetoric is an exhortation to virtue. But it is hardly logical to exhort someone to some end if the means to achieve that end are not available to him. Conservative rhetoric therefore presupposes that the laws and the institutions of the regime are good. It is precisely to the extent that the laws are bad—contemptible—that the conservative despairs of changing or reforming them: Fundamentally bad laws must have produced fundamentally bad men,

7. Actually it is not true that American conservatives believe in virtue and American liberals in freedom. Both believe in both. For conservatives freedom is literally self-government. For liberals new virtues—daring, openness, creativity—replace the old virtues.

and out of bad men do not come good laws. Which is no doubt why the *Federalist* says that the republican form presupposes a greater degree of virtue in the citizens than does any other form.

In a deeper sense, conservatism presupposes that the laws of the regime have divine sanction. The order in the souls of the citizens (their character) is a reflection of the moral universe, or ought to be a reflection of the moral universe. Radicals, on the other hand, believe that the universe is "open." The destiny of humanity, therefore, is in accordance with the destiny of the universe as a whole.

The view that the universe is "open" is the view of a historicism that has freed itself from determinism. According to this view, history is "intractable and uncontainable diversity in an open and unfinished universe."[8] In the struggle to progress, freedom "is both the means employed and the end attained."[9] "The essence of freedom is opposition to dogma."[10] Therefore: "A free society is a society in which individuals are free to define perfection and struggle toward it."[11] Because "... history teaches us that the future is full of surprises and outwits *all* our certitudes,"[12] we must resist the "temptation to define national goals in an ordered, comprehensive, and permanent way," or to "translate Americanism into a set of binding propositions."[13]


Calvin Coolidge was a student and follower of Abraham Lincoln within the tradition of American politics. The touch-stone of his rhetoric was the Declaration of Independence. The dominating goal of Coolidge's life was public service, and he consciously began his preparation for a political career as a young man. At the center of his preparation was a study of America's political history, rhetoric, and principles, particularly the principles of the Declaration.

Coolidge, born on the Fourth of July, delivered his first public oration as a young man on the Fourth. Thereafter, throughout his career, he took great care with his Independence Day addresses. Of particular note are those of 1916, 1924, and 1926.

His primary rhetorical task on those occasions he understood to be a defense of the Declaration as the ark for the eternal and noble principles of the American people. He defended it against the debunking claim that it was a relic of a past age and against the degrading claim that it was simply a document of bourgeois idealism.

8. Arthur Schlesinger Jr., *Reporter*, May 25, 1954, p. 38.
9. Arthur M. Schlesinger, Jr., *The Vital Center* (Boston: Houghton Mifflin Company, 1962), p. xvi.
10. Schlesinger, *Partisan Review*, October 1949, p. 981.
11. Ibid.
12. Arthur Schlesinger, Jr., *Encounter*, November 1966, p. 15.
13. Arthur Schlesinger, Jr., *Saturday Review*, July 14, 1962, p. 10.

Against those who believe that change is the primary phenomenon, that the universe is in ceaseless flux, that history is open, that each generation rewrites the past, that Americanism is not a set of binding propositions, Coolidge asserted the permanence of the principles of free government.

About the Declaration there is a finality that is exceedingly restful. It is often asserted that the world has made a great deal of progress since 1776, that we have had new thoughts and new experiences which have given us a great advance over the people of that day, and that we may very well discard their conclusions for something more modern. But that reasoning cannot be applied to this great charter. If all men are created equal, that is final. If they are endowed with inalienable rights, that is final. If governments derive their just powers from the consent of the governed, that is final. No advance, no progress, can be made beyond these propositions.[14]

The main target of Coolidge's rhetoric, however, was the degrading effect of the joyless quest for joy.

Statutes must appeal to more than material welfare. Wages won't satisfy, be they never so large. Nor houses; nor lands; nor coupons, though they fall thick as the leaves of autumn. Man has a spiritual nature. Touch it, and it must respond as the magnet responds to the pole. To that, not to selfishness, let the laws of the Commonwealth appeal.[15]

William Allen White said that Coolidge believed the progress of mankind would be "secreted" from the activity of the peddler and that Coolidge exalted the ideals of the captain of industry. The following is the peroration of Coolidge's address on the occasion of the one hundred and fiftieth anniversary of the Declaration of Independence.

We live in an age of science and of abounding accumulation of material things. These did not create our Declaration. Our Declaration created them. The things of the spirit come first. Unless we cling to that, all our material prosperity, overwhelming though it may appear, will turn to a barren sceptre in our grasp. If we are to maintain the great heritage which has been bequeathed to us, we must be like-minded as the fathers who created it. We must not sink into a pagan materialism. We must cultivate the reverence they had for the things that are holy. We must follow the spiritual and moral leadership which they showed. We must keep replenished, that they may glow with a more compelling flame, the altar fires before which they worshipped.[16]

---

14. Coolidge, *Foundations*, p. 451.
15. Calvin Coolidge, *Have Faith in Massachusetts* (Boston: Houghton Mifflin and Company, 1919), pp. 8-9.
16. Coolidge, *Foundations*, p. 454.

And what about the "ideals" of the great captain of industry?

> Great captains of industry who have aroused the wonder of the world by their financial success would not have been captains at all had it not been for the generations of liberal culture in the past and the existence all about them of a society permeated, inspired, and led by the liberal culture of the present. If it were possible to strike out that factor from present existence, he would find all the value of his great possessions diminish to the vanishing point, and he himself would be but a barbarian among barbarians.[17]

The fantastic material wealth of modern times is the product of modern science. Modern science is the product of liberal culture, of the great thinkers like Bacon, Newton, Descartes, and Locke. But modern life, including material prosperity, is justified only so long as it remains true to its liberal heritage, only so long as it is dedicated to the perpetuation of liberal culture and the production of liberal men. The blessings of a free republic, including the promotion of the liberal arts,

> are not to be inquired of for gain or profit, though without them all gain and all profit would pass away. They will not be found in the teachings devoted exclusively to commercialism, though without them commerce would not exist. These are the higher things of life. Their teaching has come to us from the classics. If they are to be maintained they will find their support in the institutions of the liberal arts. When we are drawing away from them we are drawing away from the path of security and progress.[18]

It is nowadays asserted that the great founders of modernity created a world in which no place was reserved for men like themselves. A corollary of this assertion is that the students of these men—the founders of modern regimes—created regimes in which no place was reserved for them.

It is said that the American regime is Lockean, i.e., based upon acquisitiveness, and was meant to be from the first. It is said that the founders of the regime, who were themselves great statesmen, having set the political system in motion believed that it would be self-perpetuating and that there would be no further need for the services of men such as themselves. They were to America as God was to Newton's universe.

The assumption of this argument is that the founders were in the decisive sense Lockeans. But we have it from Professor Leo Strauss that Locke had two political teachings, one public and one private. Unless the founders anticipated Professor Strauss by two centuries in the discovery of the private teaching,

17. Calvin Coolidge, *America's Need for Education* (Boston: Houghton Mifflin and Company, 1925), p. 35.
18. Ibid. p. 57.

then they were students of the public teaching. But the public teaching was not the teaching of acquisitiveness, or the wholesale rejection of the classical and Christian traditions. The public teaching represented Locke's teaching as a continuation and modification of what had come before.

Whatever may be said of the founders, Coolidge (following Lincoln) clearly held that the regime was not based upon selfishness or acquisitiveness and that its success depended upon the character of the citizens and especially upon the character of the statesman.

We live under the fairest government on earth. But it is not self-sustaining. Nor is that all. There are selfishness and injustice and evil in the world. More than that, these forces are never at rest. Some desire to use the processes of government for their own ends. Some desire to destroy the authority of government altogether.

Hence the need for the statesman:

So much emphasis has been put on the false that the significance of the true has been obscured and politics has come to convey the meaning of crafty and cunning selfishness, instead of candid and sincere service. The Greek derivation shows the nobler purpose. Politikos means city-rearing, state-craft. And when we remember that city also meant civilization, the spurious presentment, mean and sordid, drops away and the real figure of the politician, dignified and honorable, a minister to civilization, author and finisher of government, is revealed in its true and dignified proportions.[19]

America, for Coolidge, had not been torn away from its roots in the Western Tradition. It had grown out of that tradition and been sustained by it. Speaking at the Amherst Commencement in 1919, Coolidge made reference to the American soldiers who were returning to their studies at Amherst after service in Europe. Those soldiers, said Coolidge, "were defending their ideals, and those ideals came from the classics."

This is preeminently true of the culture of Greece and Rome. Patriotism with them was predominant. Their heroes were those who sacrificed themselves for their country, from the three hundred at Thermopylae to Horatius at the bridge. Their poets sang of the glory of dying for one's native land. The orations of Demosthenes and Cicero are pitched in the same high strain. The philosophy of Plato and Aristotle and the Greek and Latin classics were the foundation of the Renaissance. The revival of learning was the revival of Athens and Sparta and the Imperial City. Modern science is their product. To be included with the classics are modern history and literature, the philosophers, the orators, the statesmen, the poets—Milton and Shakespeare, Lowell and Whittier, the Farewell Address, the Reply to Hayne, the speech at

19. Coolidge, *Have Faith*, p. 69.

Gettysburg—it is all these and more that I mean by the classics. They give not only power to the intellect, but direct its course of action.

The classic of all classics is the Bible.

I do not underestimate schools of science and technical arts. They have a high and noble calling in ministering to mankind. They are important and necessary. I am pointing out that in my opinion they do not provide a civilization that can stand without the support of the ideals that come from the classics.

The conclusion to be derived from this position is that a vocational or technical education is not enough. We must have every American citizen well grounded in the classical ideals.[20]


This paper began with a summary of the view of some academics that the American regime is rooted in self-interest. We quoted one of the academic defenders of the regime, Martin Diamond, as saying that "If it fails to measure up to the claims of virtue, that regime may at least be easily defended from the spurious claims of idealism." There we ended the quotation. But Professor Diamond continued: "But that defense would be sorely unsatisfactory if the American regime were solely a regime of self-interest, as I have allowed it to seem . . ." Professor Diamond then went on for several pages to discuss "how the American political order rises above the unholy level of mere self-interest." In the first place, said Diamond, the regime rises to the level of enlightened self-interest, to the level of the bourgeois virtues, which are at least forms of the true virtues. More than that "it requires and tends to generate the virtues appropriate to republican self-government." Still higher yet, the American regime, while denying the claim of excellence to rule, "did not deny the unequal existence of excellences, nor the praiseworthiness of those excellences." Finally, America supplies "a not inhospitable home to philosophy."

It is true that a system of free government and free enterprise cannot persist in a moral vacuum. And in fact, free enterprise capitalism, freed from the moral restraints of reason or revelation, quickly becomes a monster. One impulse in the human soul—the acquisitive—becomes grotesquely swollen out of proportion to the other, nobler impulses. But modern democracy does not arise out of the licentious impulses in the human soul. It arises as a response to arbitrary or artificial rule. It does not reject human excellence or virtue. On the contrary: It presupposes that a free people is capable of governing itself only if it is composed of free men who are capable of governing themselves. It rejects equally the apolitical passion of the materialist and the apolitical passion of the utopian. It is public-spirited. But it does not regard public-spiritedness as the ultimate end of human life. The political sphere, like the human soul, is not

20. Ibid., p. 186.

self-contained. It is open to the divine. "Those who mold the human mind have wrought not for time but for eternity." Democratic men do not always live up to democratic ideals. Evil can never be eradicated from the human soul. But free government, seen through the pronouncements of its most authoritative defenders, raises a standard to which both the honest and the wise may repair.

# 8

# PRINCIPLES AND PHRASES

## The Place of Rhetoric in the Statesmanship of Winston Churchill

### L. P. ARNN

It is among the most persistent, and perhaps the most telling criticisms of Winston Churchill that he was a slave to his own demagoguery. Those who know anything about him know that he was a master of rhetoric. He was a compelling speaker and a compelling writer, whose force and persuasiveness in those arts kept him for several decades in the forefront of British politics.

John F. Kennedy, when he presented to Churchill his honorary American citizenship, said that Churchill had "mobilized the English language and sent it into battle." Indeed, for five years during the second world war Churchill's speeches were broadcast all over the allied, and much of the axis, world. His deep, resolute voice stirred the hearts and buttressed the spirits of millions. With the strength of his articulation he kept his country in the war, he welded a Grand Alliance of previously aloof or antagonistic nations, and he steered the free world out of despair to victory.

This unprecedented accomplishment was more than four decades in the preparation. When Churchill's long career was done his books—all concerned with politics, none irrelevant to the politics of his day—numbered more than thirty. His contributions to the press numbered more than five hundred. His collected speeches, virtually all of which were carefully, almost tediously toiled over by Churchill himself, fill more than eight thousand large crowded pages.

His official memoranda, many of which are finely crafted rhetorical documents, defy enumeration. Here was a statesman who never ceased, even during the busiest periods of administration, to argue, to cajole, to encourage the public to adopt the attitudes and the policies that he favored. Here was a statesman who knew and used the power of the word as none had done before, or have done since.

There are furious controversies that storm around Churchill's place in history. It is appropriate that his rhetoric should sit near their convergence, that historians should make his use of rhetoric a crown with which to adorn his reputation, or a stick with which to beat it.

Churchill, common historical opinion[1] would have it, was an instinctive more than a calculating politician. He was animated by the splendor of the movement, by the promise of celebrity, by the opportunity to stage a grand scene. His speeches were elaborate productions meant to stir up the audience and to win him acclaim. He himself was swept along as completely as the throng, and his own judgment was clouded as darkly as the mass he attempted to incite. There was a genius in him, but it was a fanciful, romantic, loose genius shaped and directed by the chance factors that surrounded him. His constancy of purpose sometimes exceeded all bounds, but when he was stubborn, it was in a cause that had no justification outside his own elevation, his desire to be near the cause of a big effect.

The testimony to these unfortunate traits in Churchill is to be found in the diaries, letters and books of several of Churchill's associates, and in the established historical scholarship.

Neville Chamberlain, whose place Churchill took to become Prime Minister, was for more than fifteen years a competitor with Churchill for the second position in the Conservative Party. He had abundant opportunity to examine Churchill's character, and he wrote what has become the characteristic explanation of it. In 1928 Chamberlain wrote confidentially to Lord Irwin, who was then Viceroy of India, and later (as Lord Halifax) Foreign Secretary:

> One doesn't often come across a real man of genius, or perhaps appreciate him when one does. Winston is such a man and he has *les défauts de ses qualités*. To listen to him on the platform or in the House is sheer delight. The art of the arrangement, the unexpected turn, the mastery of sparkling humour, and the

---

1. Currently, scholarship on Churchill is in an unusual state. The multivolume biography that has been written principally by Martin Gilbert is authoritative. Its authority, however, is by no means everywhere recognized. The work of A. J. P. Taylor, of Robert Rhodes James, and of most eminent historians, differs markedly in method, in interpretation, and, in some respects, in presentation of the underlying facts, from Gilbert's. Gilbert's biography supplies the evidence from which the disputes about Churchill can be arbitrated. Anyone who wishes to write on Churchill must drink from Gilbert's well. We will do so many times in what follows.

torrent of picturesque adjectives combine to put his speeches in a class by
themselves. Then as you know there is no subject on which he is not prepared
to propound some novel theory and to sustain and illustrate his theory with
cogent and convincing arguments. So quickly does his mind work in building
up a case that it frequently carries him off his own feet.

I have often watched him in Cabinet begin with a casual comment on what
has been said, then as an image or simile comes into his mind proceed with
great animation, when presently you see his whole face suffused with pink his
speech becomes more and more rapid and impetuous till in a few minutes he
will not hear of the possibility of opposition to an idea which only occurred to
him a few minutes ago.

In the consideration of affairs his decisions are never founded on exact
knowledge, nor on careful or prolonged consideration of the pros and cons.
He seeks instinctively for the large and preferably the novel idea such as is
capable of representation by the broadest brush. Whether the idea is practica-
ble or impracticable, good or bad, provided he can see himself recommending
it plausibly and successfully to an enthusiastic audience, it commends itself to
him ...[2]

Charles Masterman, who was undersecretary to Churchill in the Home
Office from 1909-12, believed that he noticed the same qualities and the same
defects in Churchill.

In nearly every case, an *idea* enters his head from outside. It then rolls around
the hollow of his brain, collecting strength like a snowball. Then, after
whirling winds of *rhetoric*, he becomes convinced that it is *right*; and denounces
everyone who criticizes it. He is in the Greek sense a Rhetorician, the slave of
the words which his mind forms about ideas. He sets ideas to Rhetoric as
musicians set theirs to music. And he can convince himself of almost every
truth if it is thus allowed once to start on its wild career through his rhetorical
machinery.[3]

Anyone who crossed swords with Churchill—and there were veritable
multitudes who did—had to cope with his extraordinary facility with words.
This facility, it could not be denied, was a mark of genius. But it seemed a
flawed sort of genius. "He handles great subjects in rhythmical language,"
admitted Lord Esher, "and becomes quickly enslaved by his own phrases."[4]

"The applause of the House," wrote Lloyd George, "is the very breath of

2. Martin Gilbert, *Winston S. Churchill*, Volume V, *The Prophet of Truth*, 1922-39, (Boston:
   Houghton Mifflin, 1977) p. 297.
3. Quoted in Robert Rhodes James, "The Politician," in A. J. P. Taylor, *Churchill Revised: A Critical
   Assessment* (New York: The Dial Press, 1969) p. 71.
4. Lord Esher to Sir Douglas Haig, 30 May 1917, printed in Martin Gilbert's, *Winston S.
   Churchill*, Volume IV, *The Stricken World*, 1916-1922 (Boston: Houghton Mifflin, 1975) p. 21;
   This passage is also quoted in Rhodes James, "The Politician," p. 79.

his nostrils. He is just like an actor. He likes the limelight and the approbation of the pit."[5]

"He has not studied to make himself a demagogue," wrote G.W. Steevens. "He was born a demagogue, and he happens to know it. The master strain in his character is the rhetorician."[6]

"The hollow" of Churchill's brain was a vessel for collecting bits and scraps of public opinion, of "ideas" floating in the air. Within that hollow vessel wild motion was imparted to those ideas. That explains the energy that Churchill brought to every matter with which he dealt. That explains his uncontrolled leaps across parties and outside parties. That explains his ability to remain for years at a time an important parliamentary figure, even without an organized or extensive circle of parliamentary friends. He was entertaining. He was enticing. He was a showman who at any moment might dart away with public opinion to some novel and unpredictable place.

Historians have found most persuasive this critique of Churchill's persuasive powers. A. J. P. Taylor, whose opinion is by itself nearly sufficient to establish historical orthodoxy, has written:

Churchill used words as weapons and was also enslaved by them. He took Macaulay's rhetoric and his own as reality and often sacrificed human beings for the sake of glittering phrases.[7]

Robert Rhodes James, historian of Churchill College, Cambridge and Member of Parliament, believes that Charles Masterman's judgment of Churchill's rhetoric had "much truth in it."[8] For Rhodes James, "the rhetorical approach" that Churchill adopted is not an approach necessarily connected with statesmanship. To be rhetorical is, in his understanding, to forego dialectics and instruction. It is to take little or no heed of views other than one's own. It is to be always "telling" others, not arguing with them, and certainly not learning from them. Rhodes James writes:

Churchill's principal failing as a politician was one of communication. To quote Lady Asquith again: "Armies are just as necessary in politics as in war. And they can only be recruited by persuasion." Churchill's essentially rhetorical approach, and the fixity with which he adhered to a point when he had carefully considered it, gave neither his public speaking nor his private conver-

5. Quoted in Rhodes James, "The Politician," p. 65.
6. G. W. Steevens, "The Youngest Man in Europe," in Eade, Charles, *Churchill by his Contemporaries* (London: Hutchinston, 1953) p. 65; This passage is also quoted in Rhodes James, "The Politician," p. 69.
7. A. J. P. Taylor, "The Statesman," in A. J. P. Taylor, *Churchill Revised* (New York: Dial Press, 1969) p. 59.
8. Rhodes James, "The Politician," p. 71.

sation the impression of a dialogue. As Morley once commented: "Whereas Winston knows his own mind, Lloyd George is always more concerned to know the minds of other people." It is sometimes difficult to decide whether this was Churchill's outstanding virtue or one of his major deficiencies; but it certainly gave him a remoteness from his audience which was often unfortunate.[9]

These attributes, Rhodes James admits, made Churchill something other than an ordinary demagogue. He was not simply a slave of public opinion; he was willing to hold a view for a long time even though it was out of favor. Once he got hold of a notion he kept it, or it kept him, through many adversities.

But still Churchill was unable to exercise judgment independently of the circumstances surrounding him. Rhodes James writes:

His independence was the independence of the adventurer and the opportunist. Until the 1930s it is difficult indeed to see in him the pursuit of any identifiable cause. But he was not one for making long-term calculations. Ardent in the pursuit of the immediate, he often neglected the future. In view of his warnings of 1912-19, 1934-39, and 1946-48, this may appear an unfair comment. But in all these cases he was drawing public attention to actual rather than hypothetical situations; his achievement—not to be disparaged by any means—was in diagnosis rather than in prognosis. It is in no way to belittle his formidable intellect to state that it was principally applied to the meeting of immediate situations rather than with anticipating future ones. What was often ascribed to recklessness was in fact the consequence of this aspect of his character. In domestic politics, this failure to illuminate the future or to envisage a new and changed society was not an advantage; it also goes far to explain why he leaves no message and no vision for the new rising generation today.[10]

This statement is typical of the established historiographical opinion of Winston Churchill. It is littered with disclaimers: nothing in it, it protests, is meant to depreciate Churchill's abilities. Indeed, it asserts that those abilities were "formidable." But its final judgment is absolute: Churchill leaves no message; he was a man of his time and of his time only. A little later in this passage Rhodes James writes: "if the British Empire were to die, it was right that it should have had a blaze of glory; be commanded by a man who would not realize that its great days were past, and who, by this belief, made others believe it as well."

Churchill's strength derived more from what he did not know, than from what he did; more from his blindness than from his vision. To study him, then, is to engage in a pleasant entertainment. It is certainly not, however, to find an example after which to pattern one's politics. There is no guidance to be derived from that historical curiosity, Winston Churchill. His very rhetorical powers are

9. Ibid, p. 126.
10. Ibid, p. 127-28.

the primary evidence that his life was ever dominated by the present and his own place in it.

Of course, there is every possibility that this historical judgment is correct. But we are reluctant to accept it without examining certain implausibilities that are apparent on its surface. Is it true, for example, that Churchill was seeing an actual, and therefore (we presume) apparent, situation when he warned of Hitler's aggression? Why then was the situation not apparent to others? Why were there so few who joined in voicing these warnings?

Is it true, for example, that because the British Empire fell, it fell *necessarily*, and *deservedly*? Is it true that because Churchill worked for its preservation, and mourned its decline, he was blind to the future?

Is it true that the legacy of a statesman depends on his envisaging "a new and changed society." Or is the hallmark of the prudent statesman a deep appreciation of the conditions that actually prevail, a wise opinion of the course that should be plotted through them, relying upon a strong sense of the final object of the journey?

Is it true, finally, that the cultivation of rhetorical ability, the adoption of "the rhetorical approach," imposes an artificial limit upon statesmanship? Is it true that the rhetorical statesman sacrifices his vision in favor of persuasive force?

A sufficient account—which we do not propose to give here—of Winston Churchill's statesmanship would answer these questions. What we will hope to do, through an examination of Churchill's early writings on rhetoric, is shed some light upon them, and indicate how Churchill himself might have answered the eminent historians who have charge of his reputation. We believe they misunderstand something about the purpose of rhetoric in general, and of Churchill's own rhetoric, in particular.

Churchill, it is true, made the most careful preparation over many years to become the speaker he was. In 1896, when he was in India, and embarked upon a course of reading that formed the basis of his education, the practical study of rhetoric was a significant part of his curriculum. He had already sat many times in the gallery of the House of Commons, absorbed as his father, Lord Randolph, grappled with Joseph Chamberlain and Gladstone and Sir William Harcourt. He was present even during the great Ireland debate of 1888, one of the most splendid outpourings of eloquence in parliamentary history.[11]

While in India, he ordered from his mother back volumes of the *Annual Register*, which contain lengthy summaries of major speeches in the major debates of every parliamentary session. With the aid of the *Annual Register*,

---

11. W. Churchill describes this occasion in Chapter III of *My Early Life* (Glasgow: Fontana Books, 1959) p. 42-43.

Churchill began to formulate in speeches—prepared as if for delivery in the Commons—his own position on the supreme questions of the day.

On March 31, 1897, he wrote to his mother from Bangalore:

... The method I pursue with the *Annual Register* is [not] to read the debate until I have recorded my own opinion on paper of the subject—having regard only to general principles. After reading I reconsider and finally write. I hope by a persevering continuance of this practice to build up a scaffolding of logical and consistent views which will perhaps tend to the creation of a logical and consistent mind.[12]

The scaffolding that Churchill was seeking to build took on a more definite shape when he wrote an essay called "The Scaffolding of Rhetoric," probably at the end of 1897. It begins:

Of all the talents bestowed upon men, none is so precious as the gift of oratory. He who enjoys it wields a power more durable than that of a great king. He is an independent force in the world. Abandoned by his party, betrayed by his friends, stripped of his offices, whoever can command this power is still formidable....[13]

There is much in this beginning, and in what follows, that is prophetic of the rest of Churchill's career, and of the historical judgment of it. "Abandoned by his party, betrayed by his friends. . ." was a condition in which Churchill was to find himself more than once. And in each case his return to power was dependent upon his ability to sway crowds and to convince the House of Commons. He had an extraordinarily independent political career; it could not have been so without his rhetoric.

But did he place his stock too completely in this art? "Of all the talents bestowed upon men, none is so precious as the gift of oratory." Churchill could hardly have assigned more importance to what he then goes on to admit is an instrument of power, relying for its effectiveness upon "human weakness," upon appeals to sentiment and emotion. The orator that Churchill goes on to describe seems not so much a guide as a manipulator.

The orator is, Churchill explains, a partly made and a partly born manipulator. The art of rhetoric, like other arts, has certain fundamental elements that can be learned, and Churchill names and describes several of them.[14] Good

12. Randolph Churchill, *Winston S. Churchill, Companion Volume II, Part I* (London: Heinemann, 1967) p. 746.
13. Ibid, pp. 816-821.
14. In the third paragraph of "The Scaffolding of Rhetoric" Churchill mentions that the main questions pertaining to rhetoric have been "revolved" "from the days of Aristotle." Much of what Churchill proceeds to write about rhetoric is strikingly similar to what Aristotle writes in

rhetoric is made of well chosen words, words that are short and are venerable elements of the language. Good rhetoric, like good music, has cadence and rhythm strong enough to carry the audience along. Near the end of a presentation, the good rhetorician will begin quickly to pile up arguments, to produce "a rapid succession of waves of sound and vivid pictures." This will serve to excite the audience, to give them glimpses of the conclusion that is to come, and to prepare "a thunder of assent" to greet the last words.

Then, the rhetorician must learn to use analogy. Analogy, Churchill writes, is a rhetorical device that "may afford a fertile theme to the cynical philosopher." It is a device that plays upon an important weakness of the auditor. Churchill writes:

> The ambition of human beings to extend their knowledge favours the belief that the unknown is only an extension of the known: that the abstract and concrete are ruled by similar principles: that the finite and the infinite are homogenous. An apt analogy connects or appears to connect these distant spheres. It appeals to the everyday knowledge of the hearer and invites him to decide the problems that have baffled his powers of reason by the standard of the nursery and the heart. Argument by analogy leads to conviction rather than to proof, and has often led to glaring error.[15]

Here, then, is a powerful and to some extent a dangerous tool of the rhetorician. Churchill calls it not a tool, but a "weapon," a single, well-chosen example of which can dominate a political issue. Its power derives from its ability to exploit an inherent or prevailing imperfection in the human being: his ignorance of many important things, and his desire to extend his partial knowledge to unknown realms. It is not a superficial, but a profound form of manipulation in which rhetoric engages.

These, then, are the tricks and instruments of the rhetorician. Their direct, though not admitted, purpose is "to allay the commonplace influences and critical faculties of his audience, by presenting to their imaginations a

---

*The Rhetoric,* especially in the third book of that work. This gives a strong indication that Churchill was familar with *The Rhetoric.* Moreover, Churchill's Headmaster at Harrow, and later friend and adviser, J. E. C. Welldon, was a translator of *The Rhetoric,* and he published his translation less than two years before Churchill became his student. In his preface to his translation, Welldon wrote: "The study of rhetoric as an education instrument ... has at least in England been practically neglected since the beginning of the eighteenth century ... It is possible that the time will come again when the world will recognize that 'it is not enough to know what to say, but it is necessary also to know how to say it'.... Then the *Rhetoric* will, I think, be widely read, as perhaps a solitary instance of a book which not only begins a science but completes it." *The Rhetoric of Aristotle,* translated (London: 1886) pp. vi, vii.

15. Randolph Churchill, *Companion Volume II,* p. 819.

series of vivid impressions which are replaced before they can be too closely examined and vanish before they can be assailed."[16]

The techniques of rhetoric are potentially tremendous weapons. But their proper use is not available to everyone. An orator is partly made, but he is also partly born. He must possess certain qualities of body, and certain qualities of soul. He must have a striking, though not necessarily a handsome, appearance. He must have a distinctive, though not necessarily a flawless, voice.[17] But more important than these physical attributes are certain attributes of character essential to the orator.

The orator must have a nature open and sympathetic to the multitude he addresses. He must be sentimental and earnest. He must, in fact, have a strong element in him that is closely akin to the passions of the throng. Churchill writes:

Indeed the orator is the embodiment of the passions of the multitude. Before he can inspire them with any emotion, he must be swayed by it himself. When he would rouse their indignation his heart is filled with anger. Before he can move their tears his own must flow. To convince them he must himself believe. His opinions may change as their impressions fade, but every orator means what he says at the moment he says it. He may be often inconsistent. He is never consciously insincere.[18]

The true orator is distinguished from the mere speaker by his mastery of certain techniques, but even more by his sympathy with the crowd. He is in one sense a manipulator, but not a detached manipulator. He himself is involved in the effect. This attribute of the orator, Churchill believes, is so essential to him that it dominates the perorations—the final, climactic moments—of most, if not all, great speeches. Churchill goes so far as to treat this attribute as an essential, redeeming, moderating feature of the art of rhetoric.

At the end of great speeches, the way has been prepared for an explosion of feeling. Step by step, the audience—*and the speaker*—have been brought to a point not only of conviction that the conclusion is true, but of passionate determination that something be done about it. The question is, how is this pent-up energy to be released?

There are two possibilities. The power of the crowd can be dissipated inside the lecture hall, in reaction to the final words of the speech. There is a tendency, Churchill writes, for great speeches to conclude with wildly extrava-

16. Ibid, p. 816.
17. Churchill, who himself had a lisp, writes: "Sometimes a slight and not unpleasing stammer or impediment has been of some assistance in securing the attention of the audience ..." Ibid, p. 818.
18. Ibid.

gant language, language so wild and extravagant "that reason recoils." Such extravagances as these achieve a two-fold and contradictory effect. Upon the crowd that hears them, there is first a burst of feeling, a boiling over of enthusiasm, but that is followed quickly by a calming of the hot passions that have been raised by the speech. The audience is quieted. The effect of the speech, which might have been explosive, is moderated. The audience will not forget what has been said, but neither will they rush out into the street to do something about it.

The immediate effect of the speech on the audience is diminished by the extreme peroration, but its longer effect, both on those who have heard the speech, and on those who will read it or hear *of* it, is dramatically amplified. The strong words of the conclusion become "the watchwords of parties and the creeds of nationalities." The slogans that let off steam for the moment serve over the longer period to win adherents and to dominate events.

That is the first method by which the passions of the throng can be released. The second is the preserve of the more violent demagogue, whose purpose is with the crowd he has before him, and with what they can do the very night of the speech. It is the method of the Mark Antony, who wishes to raise a rabble to drive Brutus from Rome. That man, Churchill writes, could best effect his purpose by drawing back from the extravagant peroration. Churchill writes:

> The orator who wished to move his audience to a deed of violence would follow his accumulative argument, his rhythmical periods, his vivid word-pictures, by a moderate and reasonable conclusion. The cooling drink will be withheld from the thirsty man. The safety valves will be screwed down and the people will go out into the night to find the expression of their feelings for themselves.[19]

This would be the method of the true tyrant, the man who wished to break up the prevailing order and establish himself as the new head and ruler. The possibility of this kind of rhetoric constitutes a serious charge against the art of rhetoric. At its perfection, when its practitioner achieves the most complete mastery, it can turn a group of tranquil citizens into a violent mob.

As we read of this power, as we read these concluding passages of "The Scaffolding of Rhetoric," we are made to wonder whether rhetoric itself should not be banned, or at least whether citizens should not be trained to beware of the rhetorician and his wiles. The effect of this passage is to raise the reader's guard, lest he find himself among a screaming crowd, running pell mell through the streets on an errand of rampant destruction. It is a curious image for Winston Churchill, budding practitioner of the art of rhetoric, to conjure up in his readers' minds as he embarks upon his career.

19. Ibid, p. 821.

But wait. Our fears are as quickly put to rest as they are raised. The crowd, we are assured, is fully protected from this undignified and corrupting fate. Churchill writes:

But a fortunate circumstance protects society from this danger. The man who can inspire the crowd by words, is as we have already observed, under their influence himself. Nor can he resist the desire to express his opinions in an extreme form, or to carry his argument to the culmination. But for this cunning counterpoise rhetoric would long since have been adjudged a crime.[20]

By this we are reassured. The orator, we may be thankful, has the weaknesses of his strengths, the defects of his qualities. He is too bound up with the crowd to manipulate them, except imperfectly. He can not send them "on a deed of violence" because he lacks the self-restraint necessary to do so. He is, heart and soul, a member of the crowd. He is made by them. They do not need to fear him.

Churchill emphasizes this aspect of the orator's character throughout "The Scaffolding of Rhetoric," and especially in an earlier place, where he speaks of "correctness of diction":

So powerful indeed is the fascination of correct expression that it not only influences the audience, but sometimes even induces the orator, without prejudice to his sincerity, *to adapt his principles to his phrases*. [emphasis added][21]

This last, telling phrase is prophetic of the dominant strain of criticism of Churchill himself. Throughout "The Scaffolding of Rhetoric" Churchill raises in various forms the question of the "sincerity" of the orator. Is he playing with his audience? Is he a charlatan, who harbors in his heart purposes secret from, perhaps destructive to, the crowd before him? Is he, as Churchill puts it, "real or artificial?" It is among the primary purposes of "The Scaffolding of Rhetoric" to answer this question and to answer it emphatically. The orator, Churchill insists, is sincere; he is only partly "artificial." At the moment he speaks, he means what he says. The audience of the orator — the audience of "The Scaffolding of Rhetoric," which may include future auditors of Winston Churchill, orator — can be reassured that it is not being herded or driven, by a shepherd or a wolf. It can believe the awesome figure on the podium. It can rest its confidence in his words, and therefore lend itself to the illusion that he sets out to create.

"The Scaffolding of Rhetoric" seems, at first glance, to be a rash work, in that it gives away the tricks of the magician. But upon closer examination it is itself, and in several senses, a rhetorical document. It pretends to stand back

20. Ibid.
21. Ibid, p. 818.

from the great rhetorical episodes, and to examine them calmly and abstractly. But in fact, though it cautions the audience to beware of certain things, it invites them to relax upon that aspect of the rhetorician's art most crucial to its success. "The Scaffolding of Rhetoric" provides the framework upon which a rhetoric can be built. It advises the aspiring rhetorician to develop, as it encourages the potential audience to perceive, a reliable, trustworthy oratorical countenance.

How ironic, then, that in this essay, which prepares the way for Churchill's own oratory, the way should also be prepared for the historian to penetrate Churchill's secret failing. We see him here, the young Churchill, in a shrewd and calculating fashion setting up his future listeners, cultivating the ground for those "hot-house plants," the "flowers of rhetoric." He is, in this way, thinking far down the road, to the day when he would stand up before the throng and extract that "explosion of feeling" that was, as Lloyd George said, the very "breath of his nostrils."

And yet, even as he thinks ahead, he thinks not far enough ahead. The multitude is prepared, but that final judge, history itself, can not be swayed by pretty language or clever tricks. Long before Winston Churchill made a great speech, almost before he made any speech at all, he understood that the rhetorician "adapts his principles to his phrases." The rhetorician is, as Lord Esher wrote of Churchill, "enslaved by his own phrases," or more precisely, by his desire to persuade and influence. Thus we have not only Lord Esher's testimony, but Winston Churchill's testimony, too. With his own words he passes judgment on his career and character.

That is the historical verdict on Winston Churchill. He was shrewd, undeniably shrewd. He calculated far, far ahead. But his shrewdness and calculation were not in service of ends that can have enduring impact. The explosion of rhetoric is made, and then it is gone. The thunder is heard, and then it recedes. Even if it resounds across continents, even if whole nations quiver at its power and march to its resonance, it finally, and utterly, and completely recedes. It leaves us nothing to ponder except the dim recollection of its glorious but fleeting echoes. Winston Churchill, his rhetoric exposed, can deceive us no longer.

The evidence for this verdict seems unassailable. We have the testimony of many of Churchill's contemporaries. We have the testimony of eminent historians. We have the testimony, it seems, of Winston Churchill himself. There are eyewitnesses. There is expert evidence. There is a confession. The case is open and shut.

There is something about the case, however, that is a little too neat. For one thing, if we accept it, we must believe rather worse of Churchill than Robert Rhodes James would have us do. The arrangement of the evidence, looked at one way, is more damning than Rhodes James lets on. In the essay from which we have been quoting, Rhodes James commends "The Scaffolding of Rhetoric" to our attention, and quotes its opening sentences. He does not, however, mention the passage about "adapting his principles to his phrases." This would have fit perfectly with another passage that he does quote, and which we have quoted, from Lord Esher: "He handles great subjects in rhythmical language, and becomes quickly enslaved by his own phrases." Rhodes James says that this aspect of Churchill's character has "rarely received adequate attention." We believe that he is right. We believe that Rhodes James himself does not give it adequate attention here.

It was not incumbent upon Rhodes James to mention that Churchill had used the expression "adapting his principles to his phrases." But we wonder why he did not. At first glance, it seems to make his argument immeasurably stronger. In Rhodes James' view, the rhetorician is heavily, even decisively influenced by his impulse to dominate. That impulse skews his vision. That impulse limits his usefulness, or the usefulness of his example and his teaching, to future generations. To have this confirmed in the words of Churchill would seem to add something important to this line of reasoning about the character of Churchill. Churchill was a self-made rhetorician. Churchill says that rhetoricians "adapt their principles to their phrases." Therefore, Churchill, by his own admission, adapted his principles to his phrases. The syllogism is complete and convincing. Why was it left out?

The reason, we believe, is fairly simple. It tends not to confirm, but to destroy Rhodes James' presentation of Churchill's character. The essential element of that presentation is Churchill's lack of a certain kind of sophistication. Rhodes James begins his essay by mentioning the fact that Churchill was "a career politician, a man who devoted himself for his entire adult life to the profession of politics." "Perhaps," he goes on, "this was not an advantage. Perhaps it would have been better had he worked and lived longer in a non-political environment..."[22] These opening remarks announce a theme that continues throughout the essay, and is emphasized at its conclusion. Churchill was not—as, for example, Robert Rhodes James is—a scholar-politician. He was a politician through and through. His actions were not grounded in a refined and cultured understanding, nor in enduring principle. It was hard to see in him "any specific objective in his life save that of an intense personal ambition." He had little or no contact with the larger, more permanent, non-political things. His faults follow from that aspect of his character. Not from any dishonesty or disingenuity do his failings come, but from his immersion in himself and what he is doing at the moment.

This description of Churchill is very convincing as it is stated by Rhodes James. Little wonder, with all these attributes, that Churchill was enslaved by his own phrases. But this particular kind of enslavement is less credible, when we

22. Rhodes James, p. 63.

discover that the slave—who was, after all, a slave to a part of himself—*knew*, well in advance of active political life, of the possibility of this kind of slavery. Churchill's anticipation of these future criticisms does not fit well with the unknowing character that Rhodes James describes. Churchill knew, at age 23, that rhetoricians "adapt their principles to their phrases." When we discover Churchill's early knowledge of and reflection upon this problem, which is inherent in rhetoric, he becomes a deeper student of the art than his critics depict.

This may or may not redound to Churchill's credit. After all, it is not the purpose of these critics of Churchill to convict him of a serious offense. They excuse him of wrong-doing with the same breath that excuses him from an exalted place in history. He was not, in their eyes, malicious; he was naive. His errors were unintentional. His failures were primarily of understanding and of temperament, and not so much of evil purpose.

Now we are presented with a more capable, and perhaps a more sinister figure. If Churchill was guilty of "adapting his principles to his phrases," if he said the thing that would convince, instead of the thing that he believed, he was guilty of an intentional wrong. Churchill seems to have chosen "the rhetorical approach" in full knowledge that it would restrict his ability to speak the truth, that it would compel him to prevaricate. This wrong, unless it is redeemed by some higher necessity than personal ambition, stands as a blot against his character. It can not even be excused as a crime of passion, for it was conceived, in "The Scaffolding of Rhetoric," long before those hot moments in front of the crowd in which Churchill worked his magic.

What we must conclude at this point is that Churchill was certainly a more sophisticated rhetorician than he is given credit for, at least by these critics. When he was still a young man, after he had made only one serious political speech, he wrote an essay that captures—we believe subtly and accurately—the conditions of high rhetoric. Those conditions have to do with the character of the audience and the character of the speaker, as perceived by the audience. What the speaker actually says is only one element of successful rhetoric, and not always the dominating element. We believe that Churchill thought about this, and understood its implications. We do not believe that he was caught unawares by one of the fundamental problems inherent in rhetoric: that knowing and speaking the certain truth and only the certain truth are not themselves sufficient for successful rhetoric, and at times are destructive of successful rhetoric.

What does that mean for the statesman who adopts what Robert Rhodes James calls "the rhetorical approach"? Does it mean that, in his pursuit of persuasive power, he must abandon every other goal? Is his statesmanship thereby narrowed to the horizon of the assembled many? To address that question, we may turn to another early work of Winston Churchill, a work that also is recommended by Robert Rhodes James as a source on Churchill's rhetoric. *Savrola* is the work, and it was written between 1897 and 1900, beginning only a few months after "The Scaffolding of Rhetoric" was probably completed.

*Savrola* is Winston Churchill's first and only novel. It is a political novel, a "tale of revolution in Laurania," an imaginary Republic. The character that dominates *Savrola* is Savrola, a young statesman of remarkable ability, who happens to be a revolutionary. If Savrola were not the creation of Winston Churchill, we would have to say that he *was* Winston Churchill. The resemblance is unmistakable, nor was it intended to be mistaken.

"The Scaffolding of Rhetoric" was never published, except that elements of it were lifted and embodied in the character and circumstances of Savrola. Savrola's principal weapon in his political struggles is his power with the crowd. He is a magician, and the chapter in which he makes "the best speech I have ever made" is called "The Wand of the Magician." The magician's tricks and tools are the tricks and tools described in "The Scaffolding of Rhetoric."

Savrola is depicted in a particular political situation. He is seeking to overturn a military dictatorship, a relatively mild one by today's standards, but still a government resting upon force, and not upon the consent of the governed. In the first scene of the novel, a crowd has gathered outside Parliament House, awaiting an announcement that the Constitution has been restored. The crowd is excited. It becomes more excited when it receives the first intimations that the Constitution will not be restored, that in fact the franchise will be severely restricted, and therefore the Dictator will be assured a majority in the legislature, whatever the people may think. The excitement of the crowd turns into rage when Moret, Savrola's best friend and closest colleague, steps before the crowd and cries out that they have been betrayed. He ends his impassioned speech with the call, "To your tents, oh people of Laurania!"[23]

The crowd surges forward toward the President, that is, toward the Dictator, and his Palace Guard. The Guard opens fire. Many are killed. General panic replaces the rage of the crowd, and the multitude flees. At the outset, then, we are given an example of rhetoric uncontrolled, of an orator carried away by the passion of the moment. But the result is not the result anticipated in "The Scaffolding of Rhetoric." The passions of the crowd are not vented. The crowd breaks toward the army, and the crowd is repulsed. There is an immediate, a violent, an undesirable and unintended effect from the first speech in *Savrola*.

Savrola enters in Chapter Three, which is called "The Man of the Multitude." His first public speech is designed to moderate the alarm of a small conference underway to consider the events at Parliament House. His first

23. Winston S. Churchill, *Savrola* (Bath, G. B.: Cedric Chivers, Ltd., 1973) p. 17.

private speech is to Moret. He rebukes Moret for what he has done, claiming that Moret has the blood of the dead and wounded on his head, claiming that Moret's speech was useless and could do no good. The rhetorician, then, is responsible for the actions of the crowd he addresses.

Moret explains that he was "furious" and "thought only of revolution." Moret rebukes Savrola for taking the situation too calmly. Savrola responds:

Look here, Moret: I am as young as you; I feel as acutely; I am full of enthusiasm. I, too, hate Molara more than is wise or philosophic; but I contain myself, when nothing is to be gained by giving way.[24]

Savrola, the true orator, is distinguished from his friend Moret by his self-restraint. Savrola is more passionate than the wise man or the philosopher would be, but he is less passionate, or less ungoverned in his passion, than Moret. This seems to be a direct contradiction of what is said in "The Scaffolding of Rhetoric." The true orator is self-restrained. "The Man of the Multitude" does not "let himself go" unless there is something to be gained by it. He is not completely "of the multitude." He can control himself in the face of mass excitement. In the person of Savrola, the "man of the multitude," we meet a man who can control his perorations; who could, if he wished, send the crowd storming into the street. At the end of the great speech in the chapter called "Wand of the Magician," Churchill writes:

For five minutes everyone shouted wildly; the delegates on the platform mounted their chairs and waved their arms. At his suggestion the great crowd would have sallied into the streets and marched on the palace; and it would have taken many bullets from the soldiers. . .to bring them back to the squalid materialities of life.[25]

Savrola could have sent them "on a deed of violence." He did not. He did not—not because he could not—because he *would* not. It was his moderation, not his passion, that moderated the effect of his speech.

The rhetorician in *Savrola* can control himself, but can he control the crowd? Once he has set the juggernaut rolling, it is not enough that he should be able to leap away to safety, abandoning the massive vehicle as it careens wildly toward destruction. The orator should know, before he raises the tempest, that he can control its blowing. Savrola is engaged in revolution-making, and revolution-making is an ambiguous and problematic enterprise. Molara, the Dictator, is a hard man, but not evidently a cruel or bestial man. There are, for example, no instances of torture in *Savrola*. Savrola, an enemy of the State, is allowed to walk freely through the capital, and to address large gatherings, to

24. Ibid, PP. 36-7.
25. Ibid, p. 121.

whom he openly ridicules the Dictator. The Dictator is therefore somewhat lenient. In fact, the Dictator, who has delivered the State from the danger of conquest, and who is a brave and able commander, has promised gradually to restore the constitutional democracy. The franchise that he announces in the opening scene, at which Moret was enraged, was a small step in that direction.

It is possible to imagine not only a better, but also a worse government for Laurania than Molara's government. Churchill the novelist does not fail to describe what a worse government might be like. There is a movement, a secret, radical movement situated on the extreme left of Savrola's party. It is a movement composed of people who are perfectly capable of envisaging "a new and changed society." In fact it is a complete transformation of society for which they aim.

These radicals are communists, and they form in *Savrola* the principal opposition to Savrola's leadership of the democratic movement. They are introduced to us by Savrola himself, in Chapter VI, which is called "On Constitutional Grounds":

"Moret," said Savrola with strange earnestness, "we have settled that. There are other things to talk about. I am troubled in my mind. There is an undercurrent of agitation, the force of which I cannot gauge. I am the acknowledged leader of the party, but sometimes I realise that there are agencies at work which I do not control. That secret society they call the League is an unknown factor. I hate that fellow, that German fellow, Kreutze, Number One, as he styles himself ... when I can no longer restrain and control, I will no longer lead.[26]

Savrola, we have already learned, "hates" Molara. He also "hates" Kreutze. He feels as strongly about Kreutze as about Molara. There is a faction within Savrola's own party that is at least as evil, perhaps more evil, than Molara's government. After Savrola gives his triumphant speech, in the chapter called "Wand of the Magician," a revolutionary named Karl, who proves to be Karl Kreutze, engages a comrade in the following dialogue as the crowd is dispersing:

"Brave words, Karl," said one.
"Ah," said the other, "we must have deeds. He [Savrola] is a good tool to work with at present; the time will come when we shall need something sharper."
"He has great power."
"Yes, but he is not of us. He has no sympathy with the cause. What does he care about a community of goods?"
"For my part," said the first man with an ugly laugh, "I have always been more attracted by the idea of a community of wives."
"Well, that too is part of the great scheme of society."

26. Ibid, pp. 70-71.

"When you deal them out, Karl, put me down as part proprietor of the President's [wife]."[27]

This Karl Kreutze becomes, near the end of the novel, the only man to drive Savrola to "ungovernable passion." Karl takes charge of the democratic forces assaulting the Presidential Palace and leads them first to victory, and then to the shooting of the Dictator. Karl inflicts the mortal wound himself, as the President lies wounded and helpless. Savrola arrives upon the scene to denounce Karl and to strike him with a cane. His reaction is the reaction of a man who sees his life's work being corrupted.

Savrola is named in several places as the creator of the movement for reform. It was his power with the crowd that gave coherence and force to the dissatisfaction with the government. The question is, will Karl Kreutze and his extremist views inherit the revolution that Savrola has begun. Can Savrola restrain, as well as incite, the crowd? In the words of Savrola:

"Look out over the city," he said. "It is a great mass of buildings; three hundred thousand people live there. Consider its size; think of the latent potentialities it contains, and then look at this small room. Do you think I am what I am, because I have changed all those minds, or because I best express their views? Am I their slave? Believe me, I have no illusions, nor need you."[28]

Savrola would seem to be placing himself in a highly questionable position. In order to challenge what seems to be a moderately bad government, he stirs up passions that may be used to form a worse government.

He is, however, at least partially excused by an important mitigating factor: Savrola himself is at least partly responsible for the Dictator's moderation. Without the power of Savrola, without Savrola's rhetoric, the hands of the Dictator would be unrestrained. The Dictator's secretary, Miguel, suggests in one place that Savrola be assassinated, and in another that he be tortured. The Dictator refuses, but only because the people would not stand for it, because "it would mean a revolution here, and close every asylum abroad." The Dictator was willing to have his wife compromised with Savrola in order to destroy Savrola, and he deliberately sends her to see Savrola in the hope that this will happen. He admits to himself that he loves his wife more when he realizes what use she is to him, than at other times. The Dictator has no appreciation of beauty for its own sake. Beautiful and good things have merit in his eyes to the extent that they are useful to him.

To the Dictator, everything is instrumental to his purpose. His purpose is to stay in office. Of flight and exile he is abhorrent: "He would not think of it; he

27. Ibid, p. 122.
28. Ibid, p. 72.

would die first; nothing but death should drag him from the palace, and he would fight to the last." A man of this temper is not someone to trust in a place of absolute authority. Savrola's movement, Savrola's rhetoric, is the principal check upon Molara's power.

Savrola's dilemma is this. His movement is a restraint upon the Dictator. Yet the forces he calls forth are themselves difficult to restrain. If they break loose from his control, an even worse situation may develop than the situation under Molara.

The action of the novel does little to dispel Savrola's dilemma. *Savrola* ends both happily and unhappily. Its literal conclusion presents Savrola, happily and honorably married to Molara's wife, ruling over a peaceful and prosperous Laurania. There is something about this ending that is a little too good to be true. We are issued a warning of this in the last sentence, in which Churchill quotes Gibbon: "history is 'little more than the register of the crimes, follies and misfortunes of mankind.'"

This happy ending is presented in a form similar to an epilogue. It fills only the last page of the novel and is separated from the rest of the novel by a break in the action. The action of the novel concludes on the penultimate page. The action of the novel ends with the revolution turning away from Savrola to Karl; with it seeking to execute summarily Molara's soldiers, after they had surrendered under promise of fair trial; with it seeking to arrest Savrola and deliver him up to Molara's Admiral for execution. Savrola flees the city, in company with Molara's wife, over a route and by a method designed for Molara's escape. As Savrola looks back on the city, he sees the Admiral open fire with his ship's guns, and the city begins to burn. "And that," said Savrola, "is my life's work."

Savrola is, then, unable to restrain the crowd, and Karl and his communists are at least immediately the inheritors of the revolution that Savrola had begun, and that—because of his rhetorical prowess—only Savrola could have begun. This would seem, once again, to constitute a profound remark by Churchill upon the efficacy of "the rhetorical approach." It can stir up trouble, but it can not moderate and guide.

It would seem, once again, that Churchill is indicating his knowledge of the limitations of "the rhetorical approach." This time, he speaks not directly, as in "The Scaffolding of Rhetoric," but through the opaque window of a novel, which portrays the failure of its hero, "The Man of the Multitude." We believe, in fact, that *Savrola* is very much a book about what is possible, and what is not possible. It is a book about the glories that may be achieved through intense political action, and also about the limitations of political action, however intense. Savrola says to Moret on the eve of the revolution that every triumph must be paid for. That, we believe, is fundamentally the perspective of *Savrola*.

And yet this constitutes no indictment, in the mind of Savrola or of his creator, of "the rhetorical approach" as a method of carrying on politics. In *Savrola*, there is in fact an alternative method of carrying on politics presented. Savrola is flanked by Molara, on the one hand, and by Karl Kreutze, on the other. Both of these gentlemen are men of deeds, not of words. Molara makes only one speech, and that is a speech to soldiers about to go to battle. The bystanders, who are civilians, boo the speech when it is finished. Kreutze, after Savrola makes his great speech, grumbles that it is not speeches so much as deeds that are required.

Savrola's political position is somewhere in between Kreutze and Molara, differing from each of them in different ways, and from both of them in some of the same ways. One of the ways in which he differs from both of them is in his adoption of "the rhetorical approach." The rhetorical approach is a tool of a certain kind of politics, of Savrola's kind of politics.

We may see this by taking another look at a part of the action of *Savrola*, the part of the action that precedes and sets the stage for Savrola's great speech, "the greatest speech I ever made." At the time of the speech, Savrola is facing two problems, or rather, two aspects of the same problem, within his own movement. His movement has a tendency toward extremism. The more dramatic aspect of the tendency toward extremism is represented by Karl Kreutze and his comrades. But they are dangerous precisely because the movement as a whole, the rank and file of Savrola's followers, has a tendency toward extremism.

In the chapter called "On Constitutional Grounds" Savrola confides to Moret his fears about Karl and his comrades. The discussion of Karl is preceded and succeeded by another discussion, a discussion of whether Savrola will attend the State Ball. Savrola has already declined an invitation from Molara to attend the Ball, which is a customary event of State. But now Savrola receives an invitation from Lucile, the beautiful wife of Molara.

Savrola changes his mind, and decides to attend. He attempts to "trick himself," in his own mind, about the true causes of his reversal. But he fails. Churchill writes:

And then he began to look for reasons for changing his mind: the old established custom; the necessity of showing his followers that for the present he was in favour of constitutional agitation only; the opportunity of displaying his confidence in the success of his plans; in fact, every argument, but the true one, was arrayed against his determination.

Yes, he would go; the party might object, but he did not care; it was none of their business, and he was strong enough to face their displeasure.[29]

Savrola encounters the vehement objections of Moret, but still he goes to the Ball. He risks, and eventually he encounters, the displeasure of the people

29. Ibid, p. 67.

—his followers—in order to go. In a way, Savrola's attendance at the Ball is a subversive act. It is subversive of the movement that Savrola has himself created. It is an act of subversion undertaken in order to visit a beautiful woman. But as it turns out, it is an act of subversion in more than one way, and the beauty of the woman represents more than a personal allurement for Savrola.

Savrola arrives at the Ball to find the guests adorned with gold distinctions of rank and honour. He arrives dressed simply in black, with no badges of distinction except his own countenance. Soon after his arrival, he catches a glimpse of Lucile, who is resplendent in a fine tiara, "peerless and incomparable among women." Savrola, "democrat though he was," bows to her sovereign appearance.

Savrola, according to Molara's design, sits next to Lucile at dinner. A discussion begins of beauty, which is regarded by the Russian Ambassador as the deity in his religion. Molara, the husband of the most beautiful of women, declares that the Ambassador's idol "stands on no surer a pedestal than human caprice." The beauty of one age, he points out, is not the beauty of the next. The beauty of one place is found hideous in another. What is thought beautiful, contends Molara, is infinitely changeable. One need only observe fashion to discover this.

It is pointed out by Lady Ferol that this is the material, not the moral, understanding of beauty. The Ambassador explains that, though he ever admires beauty, it is fitting that the standard of beauty is alterable and ever altered. Every day, he continues, cells die and the molecular structure of his brain changes. Thus it is right that he should admire a different beauty on one day, than he did the day before. "You express my views in other words," says Molara.

Then Savrola interjects a speech:

"Look at that statue," said Savrola suddenly, indicating a magnificent marble figure of Diana which stood in the middle of the room surrounded by ferns. "More than two thousand years have passed since men called that beautiful. Do we deny it now?" There was no answer and he continued: "That is true beauty of line and form, which is eternal. The other things you have mentioned, fashions, styles, fancies, are but the unsuccessful efforts we make to obtain it. Men call such efforts art. Art is to beauty what honour is to honesty, an unnatural allotropic form. Art and honour belong to gentlemen; beauty and honesty are good enough for men."[30]

This speech by Savrola was followed by an uncomfortable pause, during which "Molara looked uneasy." "The democratic tone" of what Savrola had said was "unmistakable." Savrola's democracy, we learn, is a democracy founded upon an unchanging standard, a standard that determines what constitutes

30. Ibid, p. 89.

excellence or superiority, a standard unaffected by "fashions, styles, fancies." It is of the utmost importance, in considering the politics of Savrola—and we believe of his creator—to grasp the implications of this position.

This discussion at dinner is then broken off. But it is continued a few moments later, out of doors—"In the Starlight," as the chapter is entitled —between Lucile and Savrola. Savrola sits outside, beneath the stars, beside an object of beauty that he claims to admire, not for its utility to him, but for itself. This is precisely the attitude he has for the stars, too. He loves them, we learn, because they are beautiful, and because they conform in their regular movements to a mathematical, natural standard of fitness. He does not believe that "the details of man's squalid future" are placarded across the sky by the stars. He believes the stars are indifferent to man, and related to man only in their demonstration—not for man, but perceivable by man—of the standard of fitness to which man must also conform, if he is to live well.

Beauty, to be beauty, and the stars, to survive and continue their movements, must conform to a natural standard of fitness. So must man conform to a natural standard of fitness, if he is is to survive and to live well. Honesty, justice, and other virtues are the names given to certain habits or principles of action that enable men to live well together. So long as men live, they will live best by practicing these virtues. It is not open to man—not to governments, be they monarchies, aristocracies, or even democracies—to alter the fact that practicing virtues is the way to live well.

Savrola explains to Lucile, the wife of the Dictator, that he is seeking to trample down Molara's government in order to "discharge a duty to the human species." Lucile accuses him of assailing a just and firm government "for the sake of his theories." He replies that the "lines of soldiers with loaded rifles," "the Lancers I saw spearing the people in the square a week ago" are not "theories."

Savrola resists Molara with reference to a standard of fitness, of the survival of the fittest, of the right and ability of the best to excel. Molara is wrong to obstruct this right with physical force. This standard that Molara violates does not vary with societies; Savrola's fundamental opinions are not therefore derived from imaginings of "new and changed societies."

Savrola does, however, demonstrate his ability to envisage "new and changed societies." The "new and changed societies" that he envisages seem to him a prospect to be deplored. Savrola discusses with Lucile the question of technology. He explains to Lucile how "organisms imbued with moral fitness" would ultimately rise above organisms whose virtue is physical. Civilization, which is "a state of society where moral force begins to escape from the tyranny of physical forces," ultimately triumphs over barbarism. Though civilizations have risen and fallen, "the motive power, the upward tendency was constant."

And yet Savrola sees a situation developing, a "new and changed society" developing, that he fears may interrupt forever the intermittent, up and down progress of civilization. During the last stage of civilization, mankind had gathered mighty implements in its hand, implements of physical power so potent that moral force quails before it. Churchill writes:

When we have degenerated, as we must eventually degenerate, when we have lost our intrinsic superiority, and other races, according to the natural law, advance to take our place, we shall fall back upon these weapons. Our morals will be gone, but our maxims [i.e., Maxim guns] will remain. The effete and trembling European will sweep from the Earth by scientific machinery the valiant savages who assail him.
  Lucile: "Is that the triumph of moral superiority?"
  Savrola: "At first it would be, for the virtues of civilization are of a higher type than those of barbarism. Kindness is better than courage, and charity more than strength. But ultimately the dominant race will degenerate, and as there will be none to take its place, the degeneration must continue. It is the old struggle between vitality and decay, between energy and indolence, a struggle that always ends in silence."[31]

Technology, scientific weaponry, maxim guns serve at first to place civilization on a less precarious footing. But eventually the corruption, the degeneration of civilization that has been repeated "perhaps many hundred times in this world alone," will be repeated once again, for the last time. And this last time there will be no moral force, no new civilization to rise up in the place of degeneration. Modern weapons will ensure that "silence" will be the end result. "After all," said Savrola, "we could not expect human development to be constant. It is only a question of time before the planet becomes unfitted to support life on its surface."

  Lucile: "But you said that fitness must ultimately triumph."
  Savrola: "Over relative unfitness, yes. But decay will involve all, victors

31. Ibid, p. 93; cf. Winston S. Churchill, *The River War* (New York: Charles Scribner's Sons, 1935) p. 274, where Churchill describes such a scene that he had actually witnessed: "The infantry fired steadily and stolidly, without hurry or excitement, for the enemy were far away and the officers careful. Besides, the soldiers were interested in the work and took great pains. But presently the mere physical act became tedious. The tiny figures seen over the slide of the backsight seemed a little larger, but also fewer at each successive volley. The rifles grew hot—so hot that they had to be exchanged for those of reserve companies. The Maxim guns exhausted all the water in their jackets, and several had to be refreshed from the water bottles of the Cameron Highlanders before they could go on with their deadly work. The empty cartridge cases, tinkling to the ground, formed a small but growing heap beside each man. And all the time out on the plain on the other side bullets were shearing through flesh, smashing and splintering bone; blood spouted from terrible wounds; valiant men were struggling through a hell of whistling metal, exploding shells, and spurting dust—suffering, despairing, dying. Such was the first phase of the battle of Omdurman."

and vanquished. The fire of life will die out, the spirit of vitality become extinct."

Lucile: "In this world perhaps."

Savrola: "In every world. All the universe is cooling—dying, that is—and as it cools, life for a spell becomes possible on the surface of its spheres, and plays strange antics. And then the end comes; the universe dies and is sepulchered in the cold darkness of ultimate negation."

Lucile: "To what purpose then are all our efforts?"

Savrola, "cynically": "*God knows, but I can imagine that the drama would not be an uninteresting one to watch.*"[32]

Savrola has defied his followers, and risked his movement, in order to come to a Ball and admire a beautiful woman. Her beauty "thrills him." It also serves as a manifestation of the true nature of beauty, its unchanging aspect. With the beautiful woman, Savrola goes out "In the Starlight." There he explains to her his understanding of the nature of things.

His understanding of the nature of things culminates in an understanding of the way that life goes on. It goes on under the constraints of an unchanging nature, a standard of fitness that establishes, for example, honesty and justice as essential to the good life. There is nothing that man—however he governs himself, democratically or tyrannically—can do to change that fact.

It is true, however, that man is a kind of miracle worker, that he invents implements of incredible power. But with these implements, Savrola asserts, man can do no better than eventually destroy himself. Every triumph must be paid for. Man cannot radically alter his condition for the better. Civilization climbs up, and then it falls down. "New and changed societies," if they come, will be something to be decried, not celebrated.

Savrola believes in a natural standard of fitness. But he is not a progressive; he does not believe in the infinite progress of mankind. It is a happy thought that reason, the mind's eye, can discover the place of man in nature, can establish, at least in rough outline, what the best life to live is. But in Savrola's discussion with Lucile, this happy thought is offset by more dismal thoughts. The universe seems to be cooling. Mankind seems to be growing so powerful as to be able to upset the natural pattern, though not to overturn the natural constraints. "What does this mean for our lives here?" asks Lucile. God knows, responds Savrola, but it is an interesting drama to watch.

Savrola considers himself a spectator in a drama. He calls man "a consequential atom." He refers to himself as "a philosophic microbe," who is amused by the vast story he sees unfolding before him. He is not downcast by the imponderable side of existence— "if we exist at all." In fact, beside his awareness of this most radical question, the question of whether we *are*, Savrola's dismal account of the cooling of the universe appears relatively mild. Neither the most radical question, nor the cooling of the universe, nor the awesome, per-

32. Churchill, *Savrola*, p. 94.

haps uncontrollable power of modern science serves to make him despair, or to become uninterested in life. His speculations add to his amusement.

However, Savrola's speculations are emphatically not idle speculations. He is keenly interested to watch, but for him watching involves *doing*. When, for example, Savrola arrives at the State Ball, he speaks with a young lieutenant, who later helps to save Savrola's life. They speak of war and death. Savrola, who has seen no war, is stirred by the discussion. He wonders: "... one day perhaps he would open this strange book of war, and by the vivid light of personal danger read the lessons it contained." Later in the novel, Savrola deliberately exposes himself to gunfire, and is wounded. This is the highlight of a chapter called "An Educational Experience."

Personal danger, experience, the making of choices under pressure, are what exhilarate and also what educate Savrola. They shine a "vivid light" upon his life. It is true that he has learned from books. We are given a tour of his library and shown some of the books that have taught him. But the books give him lessons that have to do with life, lessons that he can comprehend only through and with reference to life. This gives moderation and balance to his more dismal speculations. Life, and the active living of it, is the touchstone against which he tests his thoughts. He says to Lucile that, if there is an afterlife, he believes it will be a better life. How does he know this? He explains: "Life, to continue, must show a balance of happiness." This he learns, not from scholarly or academic reflections, but by an intense reading by the "vivid light." Savrola is a politician through and through.

We must remember the auspices under which Savrola has this conversation in which he reveals so much about himself. He is there at the State Ball at the invitation of Lucile, the beautiful wife of the Dictator. His speeches are a kind of homage to her beauty. They impress her deeply. We are told of her, in the second chapter, that she has known and enjoyed a life of power and elegance, but that now this life is wearing thin. She has "a wistful aspiration." Savrola reveals to her a realm that she has hitherto not known. It is partly a speculative realm. It demonstrates to her, unmistakably, that Savrola is subversive through and through of her husband's government. It reveals to her that there are reasons for his subversion of which she previously had no inkling. Savrola's speeches are effective. She does not report him to her husband, not even later, when she has information that might destroy the revolution.

Savrola is also there at the State Ball in defiance of the requirements of his own movement. His own movement is restless at any display of acceptance of the opposition. The members of his movement wish to draw the line between friend and enemy straight and hard. Savrola wishes to draw the line a little less rigidly. He wishes to have the consequences of the struggle mitigated by leniency. Savrola's attendance at the Ball serves to demonstrate this. But that is not the reason why he came. He came for a private reason.

Moreover, the speeches that he makes at the Ball, and "In the Starlight," would for the most part have been entirely inappropriate as speeches in public to his own movement. He speaks with two tongues. During his great speech, his "Wand of the Magician" speech, he talks of the right, "even of the most miserable of human beings," to happiness. At the ball he speaks of standards of excellence, of standards so high that whole generations do not produce a single soul to meet them. He speaks of fashions and fancies, and their pettiness. He describes the limits that are imposed even upon democracy. He indicates, implicitly, the circumstances under which he would have to abandon his own movement, and leave the city. He predicts, implicitly, the climax of the novel.

Savrola attends the Ball, and earns the displeasure of his followers. While he is there, he says a number of things that he does not say to his followers, or does not say in the same way. At no point, however, is he disloyal to the revolution he is making. On the contrary, he states profound reasons why he is so committed, heart and soul, to the revolution. He states profound reasons why he believes that the things he says in front of the multitude are true. But a different sort of discourse is possible and appropriate in the starlight than in front of the multitude.

There are, then, two aspects of Savrola. There is the Savrola in front of the multitude, and the Savrola in the starlight. These two aspects are not, however, contradictions. They are united—their harmony is apparent—through Savrola's rhetoric. The action of the novel emphasizes this.

Savrola's great speech is given to the most difficult, the most disaffected audience that he ever addressed. The press has attacked him vehemently for attending the State Ball. Karl and his comrades have been busy agitating against him. Molara's paid agents are lurking in the crowd, ready to whip to an even greater fury the strong feeling against him. Savrola was well aware of the situation he would face. Churchill writes:

He knew he had been unwise to go: he had known from the first; and yet somehow he did not regret his mistake. After all, why should his party dictate to him how he should rule his private life? He would never resign his right to go where he pleased. In this case he had followed his own inclination, and the odium which had been cast upon him was the price he was prepared to pay. When he thought of his conversation in the garden, he did not feel that he had made a bad bargain. The damage, however, must be repaired.[33]

Savrola was compelled to choose between two things: his conversation in the garden, which was an opportunity to discuss and consider some of his dearest reflections; and the goodwill of his followers. It was a difficult choice. To give up the conversation in the garden, to give up his private life, would be to give up much of what made him worthy to be the leader of his followers. It

33. *Ibid.*, p. 103.

would be a transformation of his character. He would become, in a different sense, a politician through and through, and a lesser politician, too.

To alter the character of Savrola would be to alter the character of his movement. He was the guiding light of his movement. If he became a different leader, his movement would become a different movement. Therefore, the choice that Savrola made, the "bargain" of trading the pleasure of his followers for the conversation in the garden, was really no choice at all. There was really no separating Savrola's private life from his public life. He could not give up his private life, which his followers demanded of him, and remain the man he was, the leader he was. He was an independent man, a man with opinions that were more comprehensive and true than those of anyone else in Laurania. That caused problems with his followers. What was he to do?

There was only one thing for him to do: "the damage must be repaired." The only thing that he could do was win the followers back, and he, and only he, could do that. To do that, he would need his magic wand, "The Wand of the Magician." With that wand he could bring his followers once again under his leadership. His wand, his rhetoric, was as much an essential condition of his statesmanship as was his judgment of means and ends.

The independent statesman, the man who would think for himself and seek to do right as he sees it, will find it necessary to adopt "the rhetorical approach." Without "the rhetorical approach," he will find himself "abandoned by his party, betrayed by his friends," and he will have no tool to continue the fight. He will be ineffective. He will find it necessary—as Winston Churchill and Savrola did *not* find it necessary—to follow his party whither it leads him.

"The rhetorical approach" can take one to the very limit of what is possible through political action. It cannot surpass that limit. It need not attempt to surpass that limit. "The rhetorical approach," as Winston Churchill understood it, involves no attempt—precludes any attempt—to envisage for the public or to found "a new and changed society." It is a tool of a certain kind of statesmanship, a prudent statesmanship, instructed at once by what is best and what is possible, aware always of the dictates of nature, and the dictates of living here and now.

We would be the first to admit that this examination of "The Scaffolding of Rhetoric" and *Savrola* does not constitute a whole refutation of Churchill's critics. Those critics contend that Churchill's "rhetorical approach" was a sign that he was too much immersed in the multitude, and that his own judgment was clouded by his overwhelming desire to produce an effect upon the audience. Churchill lacked the long vision required to "envisage a new and changed society" or to "illuminate the future." Therefore, however interesting it may be to study this astonishing figure, it is hardly instructive to do so, except perhaps in a negative way.

This is a plausible case. It is supported, or seems to be supported, by the fact that Churchill toiled as few had toiled before him to master the art of rhetoric. It is supported by the fact that many people who knew Churchill well and observed him over many years said similar things about him. It is supported by the fact that Churchill himself said that the rhetorician must "adapt his principles to his phrases."

It is a plausible case. It is connected with and used to support a more general interpretation of Churchill's thought and character. It would be necessary, in order to refute this case, to undertake a general examination of Churchill's prudence as it is revealed in his deeds and his words. We have not done that here.

We have, however, discovered certain arguments in Churchill's own early writings that call the interpretation of Churchill's "revisers" very gravely into doubt. It is an entirely different thing, for example, to adapt one's principles to one's phrases, than it is to be enslaved by them. It is a matter of common sense that in politics principles have mostly an indirect, diluted relevance. They must be qualified, in their application, by circumstances, by particulars. An important circumstance or particular has to do with the opinions of the people, with what they believe. What the people believe helps to define what they will accept as advice from their leaders. The speaker, if he is prudent, will employ phrases that the audience is willing to accept. He will "adapt his principles to his phrases." To do anything else would be futile and contradictory. To do anything else would damn his cause to failure.

The prudent statesman, when he discovers a phrase that will render his position more convincing, will be pleased and excited. That pleasure and excitement is akin to the pleasure and excitement of reasoning rightly to a just and true position. Winston Churchill felt many times in his life the pleasure that attends the formulation of fine phrases. Some of his critics, seeing him in those moments, concluded that he was dominated by that pleasure.

We believe that Churchill's historian-critics, in accepting the verdict of Churchill's contemporaneous critics, have given too little weight to this aspect of rhetoric. It is only a mild caricature to portray someone who "adapts his principles to his phrases" as someone who is "enslaved by his phrases." Before the historian accepts such a characterization, which may be a caricature, he should examine very carefully the credentials of his witness. Was the witness— as, for example, Lord Esher and Neville Chamberlain were to Churchill—a political opponent of the man who is being judged? Such considerations as this will flash warning signals to the cautious historian. He will know to make allowances, because he will know that partisanship is irremovable from politics.

The brightest warning, however, must always be flashed by the subject of the historian's gaze. Winston Churchill adopted "the rhetorical approach" deliberately. His mastery of that art was superb; it may even have been supreme in modern times. That should warn the historian that he is dealing with an uncommon phenomenon.

Churchill took the trouble, at the outset of his political career, to give an account of rhetoric. Churchill's account of rhetoric, read carefully, directly contradicts Robert Rhodes James' account of Churchill's rhetoric. We would not know that by reading Rhodes James.

Churchill's arguments concerning rhetoric reveal a deep reflection upon the place of rhetoric in statesmanship. We may summarize his understanding with reference to three questions he asks near the beginning of "The Scaffolding of Rhetoric."

First, is rhetoric "born or acquired?" Churchill answers that it is both. There are certain elements of rhetoric that can be reduced to clear prescriptions, and, with patient application, can be mastered. "The flowers of rhetoric," Churchill writes in *Savrola*, "are hot-house plants." They are not wild plants growing on their own. They must be cultivated. Still, the highest accomplishments of rhetoric are available only to those born with a genius for rhetoric. In "The Scaffolding of Rhetoric," it seems that this genius consists in an affinity with the crowd. However, when the argument and the action of *Savrola* are added to this, it becomes apparent that other talents than those exercised in front of the crowd are essential to the highest rhetoric.

Second, is rhetoric "real or artificial?" This question is closely connected with the third question: does rhetoric "work for good or ill?" Churchill's answer to these questions in "The Scaffolding of Rhetoric" is somewhat different from that provided in *Savrola*. Churchill, in the former work, contends that rhetoric, being real, necessarily works for good. True oratory, true rhetoric, is possible only for the man with a deep sympathy with the crowd. In front of the crowd, artifice drops away, and the figure at the podium becomes "real," that is to say, he becomes sincere. Being sincere, he cannot deceive the audience. He is carried away in his peroration, and because of that he cannot move the crowd to a "deed of violence." Rhetoric is, because of this "cunning counterpoise," a force for good.

This account of rhetoric may be sufficient for an essay that claims to provide "the scaffolding" of rhetoric. It is not, however, the whole story as Churchill sees it. In *Savrola*, a different account is given. In *Savrola*, rhetoric is connected with the general problem of statesmanship. Its purpose is to moderate as well as to move the citizens. It requires the statesman to exercise restraint. It unites the two aspects in him, the aspect having more to do with the urgencies of the moment, and the aspect having more to do with the enduring questions posed by politics. The statesman in whom these two aspects are most truly in harmony will be—will have to be—the rhetorical statesman.